# THE JESUS EFFECT

## Dennis Hensley

# THE JESUS EFFECT

## Dennis Hensley

**Pacific Press Publishing Association**
Boise, Idaho
Oshawa, Ontario, Canada

Edited by Bonnie Widicker
Designed by Dennis Ferree
Cover by Darrel Tank
Typeset in 11/13 Century Schoolbook

Copyright © 1991 by
Pacific Press Publishing Association
Printed in United States of America
All Rights Reserved

Unless otherwise indicated, Scripture references in this book are from the New International Version.

The author assumes full responsibility for the accuracy of the facts and quotations cited in this book.

Library of Congress Cataloging-in-Publication Data:
Hensley, Dennis E., 1948–
　　The Jesus effect: achieving your personal best through Christ / Dennis E. Hensley.
　　　　　p.　　　cm.
　　ISBN 0-8163-1051-3
　　1. Christian life—1960– 2. Jesus Christ—Example. I. Title.
BV4501.2H37455　　　1991
248.4—dc20　　　　　　　　　　　　　　　91-12731
　　　　　　　　　　　　　　　　　　　　　　　CIP

# Contents

| | | |
|---|---|---:|
| Chapter | 1. Understanding the "Jesus Effect" | 9 |
| Chapter | 2. Love | 17 |
| Chapter | 3. Endurance | 24 |
| Chapter | 4. Boldness | 31 |
| Chapter | 5. Humility | 45 |
| Chapter | 6. Forgiveness | 53 |
| Chapter | 7. Communication | 62 |
| Chapter | 8. Prayer | 69 |
| Chapter | 9. Simplicity | 74 |
| Chapter | 10. Discipline | 79 |
| Chapter | 11. Vision | 84 |
| Chapter | 12. Admonition | 91 |
| Chapter | 13. Success | 99 |
| Chapter | 14. Composure | 104 |
| Chapter | 15. Mission | 117 |

# Dedication

This book is dedicated to
Henry Gariepy,
my friend and writing mentor for many years and
the man who insisted that I put my concepts of
the "Jesus Effect" on paper. Many thanks, Hank!

## Chapter One

# Understanding the "Jesus Effect"

During the 1980 Olympics, American athlete Eric Heiden took all five gold medals in men's speed skating. In the first four events, Heiden set new Olympic speed records: 38.03 seconds for the 500 meters; 1 minute, 15.18 seconds for the 1,000 meters; 1 minute, 55.44 seconds in the 1,500 meters; and 7 minutes, 2.29 seconds in the 5,000 meters. In the final event, the 10,000-meter race, Heiden not only broke the Olympic record, he also set a new all-time *world* speed record with a clocked time of 14 minutes, 28.13 seconds.

Amazing as these victories were, they came as

no surprise to observers. For many years Eric Heiden had been winning every amateur race he competed in. He was recognized as the greatest men's speed skater to have ever lived. Sports writers knew it; coaches knew it; even Heiden's competitors knew it. The plain and simple fact was, *no one could equal Eric Heiden* when it came to speed skating.

Now, you might logically think that such knowledge would be demoralizing and deflating to people who had to compete against Heiden. After all, what could be the point of entering a race when one knew in advance he had no chance whatsoever of equaling the champion? Depressing, right?

Well, actually, just the opposite proved true. When Heiden won the 500-meter race, the second-place silver medal honors went to Evgeny Kulikov of the USSR, who turned in his personal fastest time ever for the 500-meter race. When Heiden won the 1,000-meter race, the runner-up was Gaetan Boucher of Canada, who clocked his personal fastest time ever in the 1,000-meters.

And so it went in every race. The silver and bronze medalists who lost to Heiden actually achieved greater personal speeds than ever before, simply because they were doing their best to be the equal of Eric Heiden.

This phenomenon became known as the "Heiden Effect," which now is defined as "achieving new personal victories by striving to equal a competitor one knows he can never be equal to or surpass."

As Christians, we, too, are to run a good race and finish our course (see 2 Timothy 4:7). And like the

Olympic skaters, we need someone to hold up as the ultimate example so that we can rise to the challenge and achieve our best possible performance.

We have such an example in Jesus. Just as the Heiden Effect motivated the Olympians, the "Jesus Effect" can motivate dedicated Christians.

Whereas it is true we can never equal Jesus on any level, just making the effort to be like Him will raise us to new measures of purity. We are admonished to "make every effort to be found spotless, blameless and at peace with him" (2 Peter 3:14).

Naturally, there is only One who truly is without spot and blameless. Try as we may, we'll never equal Him. But try we must, nevertheless. The effort alone will bring out the best in each of us.

## Gauging the pacesetter

In our race through life on the road to heaven, we are instructed to run flat-out, putting forth a championship effort. Paul wrote, "Do you not know that in a race all the runners run, but only one gets the prize? Run in such a way as to get the prize" (1 Corinthians 9:24).

If you feel weary or weak, as though you need to fall back and slow down, look ahead to Jesus. He will be out front, setting the pace. Strive to draw up behind Him. After all, Moses looked on the back of God, and his countenance was changed (see Exodus 33:20-23).

Let's consider just five of the specific ways in which we can strive to equal Jesus.

*Love.* Jesus gave everything to prove His love for

us—even His life (see John 3:16). Surely in comparison to this, we should be able to show patience, friendship, affection, and brotherly concern for our fellow human beings. Jesus usually does not call us to sacrifice our lives as He did, but He *has* called us to love one another as He loved us (see John 15:12, 17).

In January 1982, an Air Florida Boeing 737 faulted in its liftoff from National Airport in Washington, D.C. The plane crashed into the Fourteenth Street Bridge, tearing the tail section from the fuselage, before plunging into the ice-covered Potomac River. Horrified commuters on the bridge watched the fuselage disappear through a hole in the ice. Shortly, five passengers and a stewardess were seen clinging to the still-floating tail section.

A rescue helicopter dropped a lifeline to the survivors. One man passed the lifeline to a woman next to him, allowing her to be pulled up first. A second time the lifeline was lowered, and the second time the man passed it to someone else. The procedure continued until the other five were pulled to safety. Finally, the helicopter returned for him. This time, however, it was too late. While the fifth person was being lifted to safety, this unselfish hero had slipped beneath the frigid water. Ironically, none of the five survivors knew the man's identity, much less were they his friends or relatives.

Christians who keep their eyes set on Jesus can learn to act nobly and self-sacrificially. The love Christ showed to us is a standard worth emulating.

*Endurance.* Jesus was not a quitter. He endured the deprivation of a forty-day fast in the desert and still was able to defeat Satan. He was able to endure the scourge of the whip and the nails of the cross, yet still complete His holy mission on earth. In light of this endurance, do we dare say that *anything* He calls us to do is too difficult or too demanding? Surely not. We must learn to "endure hardship . . . like a good soldier" (2 Timothy 2:3). Jesus set the example for ultimate endurance.

When my children were small, they would often ask me to help them complete a major project they had started. At first their enthusiasm for building a birdhouse or planting a flower bed would run high. However, after half an hour of sawing boards or shoveling dirt, they would tire of the project. Their mental vision of the completed project no longer merited the effort required to endure to its completion.

Unfortunately, some Christians behave similarly. As long as their lives are running smoothly and their imagined futures look rosy, they can be faithful to the disciplines of their Christian beliefs. However, if things become rough and require an element of endurance, they often are ready to quit. Christ set an example of endurance for us to follow. Such enduring faith warrants a faithful endurance.

*Boldness.* Jesus was never fearful of proclaiming the truth. At age twelve He debated the elders in the temple. As an adult, He upset the tables of the money-changers and drove them from the house of God. As an evangelist, He met the challenges of the lawyers and priests and rabbis. He spoke the truth, lived the truth, defended the truth. With Him as our example, we too must boldly proclaim to those we meet in this world the truth that Jesus Christ is the Son of God and by His shed blood we all can be redeemed (see John 14:6).

Often the simplicity of truth can embolden its proclamation. In Hans Christian Andersen's story "The Emperor's New Clothes," it took a child to say aloud that the emperor had on no clothes at all before everyone else would admit that they, too, saw no clothes on the emperor.

How similar this is to the simplicity of a truthful life before God. There is a quiet boldness in the actions of a person who does not defile his or her body or mind in the carnality of the world. When one credible person stands boldly for the truth, others are bound to notice.

*Compassion.* Jesus came to save all people. When He looked over Jerusalem and considered how many people would choose to die without accepting the salvation He offered, it broke His heart and He wept (see John 11:35). His deepest desire is for everyone to repent and not perish in sin (see 2 Peter 3:9). His limitless compassion reaches out to the sick, the blind, the young, the morally corrupt, the poor, the outcasts, the weak—all precious to Him. Such compassion should melt our hearts, humble us, and give us a burden for lost people.

During a large faculty gathering at Harvard, Albert Einstein found himself next to a high-school student, the son of a Harvard professor. "Excuse me," said the boy, "but you look like the famous Professor Einstein. Are you?"

The old scientist smiled and responded, "If you have to ask, then I'm not nearly as famous as you might think."

Such a lack of arrogance and a concern for the feelings of others marks the compassion of a follower of Christ. Christ chose to approach human beings in a meek and gentle way, hiding His power and glories. His compassion for their needs sets a standard for us.

*Forgiveness.* Peter asked Jesus how often an offender should be forgiven. Peter suggested seven times as a maximum. Jesus suggested seventy times seven as a starting point (see Matthew 18:22). Fortunately for Peter, Jesus had such a great range of forgiveness, because Peter needed forgiveness from the Lord far more than seven times.

From the night he failed to walk on the sea because he took his eyes off Jesus until the night he three times denied even knowing Jesus, Peter was a terrible offender to the Lord. Yet, because Jesus was long-suffering and forgiving, He was able to develop Peter into one of the most dynamic evangelists of the early church.

Are we any better than Peter? Certainly not. Then how can we expect God to forgive us for our continual sins? There's only one way: we can accept the forgiveness that Jesus freely offers (see 1 John 1:9). While forgiveness is an unmerited gift, we *can* do something to prepare our hearts to receive His forgiveness. We can forgive others graciously, the way God forgives us. Jesus taught, "If you hold anything against anyone, forgive him, so that your Father in heaven may forgive you your sins" (see Mark 11:26).

So then, whatever Christian virtue we wish to develop, we have a pattern in Jesus, who was perfect in every way. To become "similar" to Him is to be more noble and sincere than we could ever have imagined possible.

The philosopher Henry David Thoreau wrote, "In the long run, men hit only what they aim at. Therefore, though they should fail immediately, they had better aim at something high."

How true, how true. And at what more righteous goal can a Christian aim than to be like Jesus! The *effect* a Christlike walk can have on a person is miraculous—for the Jesus Effect *is* the miracle of God working in us.

Let us now read how we can use the Jesus Effect to enhance our lives.

## Chapter Two

# Love

Have you ever stopped to think about what it means when someone pledges "undying love and devotion" to someone else? Because that phrase is used so casually in contemporary romance novels and TV soap operas, we have forgotten that it originally meant to be totally dedicated to the care of someone else in both life and death.

As long as he lives, Joe DiMaggio has fresh flowers sent each day to the grave of his deceased ex-wife Marilyn Monroe. Mamie Eisenhower used to make trips to the Dwight D. Eisenhower Memorial Library just to be able to walk up to the library's life-size statue of her late husband and touch its hands. The breathtaking Taj Mahal, which took fourteen years to construct, was built as a mausoleum for Shah Jahan's favorite wife. Harry Houdini wasted thousands of dollars and many years working with spirit mediums in an attempt to make contact with his dead mother.

Such amazing—often bizarre—stories as these from real life help us accept as plausible the fictional tales of *Romeo and Juliet* and *A Tale of Two Cities,* wherein undying love and devotion are portrayed. We are fascinated by the power that genuine undying love can have on people.

One of the most phenomenal examples of undying love is recorded in 2 Samuel 21:1-14. Under Saul, the Jewish army had broken a peace treaty with the Gibeonites, slaying many of their people and conquering their land. When Saul violated the covenant Joshua had made centuries before, God punished the Jews for the Gibeonites by causing a three-year famine.

When David learned the reason for the famine, he sought to make amends for the violence Saul and his army had brought against the Gibeonites. The only "payment" they would accept was blood for blood. Since Saul had killed the Gibeonite families, the Gibeonites demanded that members of Saul's family be killed in return. They asked for seven of Saul's sons or grandsons to be brought to Gibeah for execution. David had no choice but to accept their terms.

King David sent to Gibeah five of Saul's grandsons, the sons of Saul's daughter Merab; he also sent Armoni and Mephibosheth, Saul's two sons by his concubine Rizpah. These seven were executed atop a hill, where their bodies could be seen by all who passed. Following this symbolic restitution, God ended the famine in the land of Israel.

But the story does not end there.

Rizpah, the mother of two executed sons, was absolutely heartbroken over her loss. With self-sacrificing devotion and undying love, she set up a vigil over her sons' bodies, vowing not to leave until they were removed from the gallows and given a proper burial.

The hangings took place early in the harvest season. Rizpah spread a sackcloth on a rock near the gallows and kept a watchful eye on the bodies of her sons. If a bird set down on either corpse, Rizpah would hurl stones and shout to scare it away. If a wild animal crept in at night, Rizpah would wave the sackcloth to shoo the animal away.

Day after day, week after week, month after month, Rizpah kept her watch over the bodies of her sons. Harvest passed, planting time came and was followed by the returning rains, and still Rizpah's undying love for her sons kept her on duty.

Word of Rizpah's incredible vigil eventually reached King David, who immediately empathized with her loss and anguish. David negotiated the return of Saul's and Jonathan's bones for burial at Zelah in the family tomb. Then, in honor of Rizpah's continual watch, David expanded the arrangement to also include the seven corpses in Gibeah. So it was that Armoni and Mephibosheth were finally given a proper burial in Israel, and Rizpah was released from her long vigil.

What is most compelling about this fascinating story is that the events transpiring on both sides were brought about by someone's undying devotion to someone else. The love the Gibeonites had for their family members who were slain by Saul did not end at their burials. When the appropriate time arose to prove this undying love, they did so. Likewise, Rizpah's maternal devotion to her sons knew no limitations in its faithfulness. Through hot days, cold nights, bitter winds, heavy rains, and attacks by wild animals, she endured discomfort and risked her health and safety to keep her sons' bodies from desecration.

We can be impressed by these actions, perhaps even astonished. Yet they pale in comparison to the undying love Christ has for lost sinners. His love is so total that He entered this world knowing in advance that He Himself would have to bear *all* the sin for the human race's fallen generations. He knew that He would be beaten, humiliated, tortured, and crucified as an atonement for sinners.

That's difficult to comprehend. But we need to consider an even more amazing point: We can understand the Gibeonites' devotion to their slain relatives, for they may have shared many hours of mutual happiness; and we can understand Rizpah's devotion for her two slain sons, for they had loved and cared for her for many years. But what was *Christ's* motivation? Why should He die for *us*? He loved us "while we were still sinners" (Romans 5:8). *We did nothing to merit His total love*—He gave of Himself freely. Our salvation was a "gift of God"

(Ephesians 2:8). Christ's love was not precipitated by someone else showing Him love. His motivation came from a love so pure that we will never be able to comprehend it.

Fortunately, we are not required to comprehend it, only to accept it. And when we do, we experience a firsthand miracle. The miracle of being able to communicate through prayer with One who is beyond the grave—to communicate with One whose love transcends time and space. Unlike Houdini in his foolish quest for contact with his dead mother, we are in continuous contact with our living Saviour, the One who conquered death.

Rizpah's love for her dead sons was genuine, but from the moment they were executed, that love was all one-sided. She could love them with all her heart, but they were incapable of ever again returning that love to her. Christ, however, rose from the dead and continues to live. Our love for Him is two-sided, for He loves us too—actively, daily, totally.

Why? The Bible gives us a simple answer. It is because, "God *is* love" (1 John 4:8, emphasis supplied).

## Loving like Jesus

An obvious question follows: "If Jesus is pure love and we are fallen sinners, how can we even begin to love as He does?" The response is this: Despite our inability to love as deeply as Jesus loves, we can exceed our own normal limits by emulating Him.

This is done in two ways: by studying the life of Christ and trying daily to behave as He behaved, and by immersing ourselves so deeply in the Scriptures that our every action is guided by God's Word. Note the progression here:

First, we read God's Word to increase our faith in Jesus and our trust in His teachings. Romans 10:17 explains, "Faith comes from hearing the message, and the message is heard through the word of Christ."

Second, we accept the fact that Christ has paid the sin debt for our salvation, and we become motivated to live a life that honors Him. First Peter 2:24 says, "He himself bore our sins in his body on the tree, so that we might die to sins and live for righteousness; by his wounds you have been healed."

Third, we grow spiritually by reading the Scriptures and allowing the Holy Spirit to use God's Word to help us mature as Christians. John 6:63 says the Word of God is our spirit and life: "The Spirit gives life. . . . The words I have spoken to you are spirit and they are life."

Fourth, we judge and respond to each situation in life the way Jesus did—by seeing how it conforms to scriptural teachings. He quoted Scripture verses frequently as a way of explaining who He was, why He behaved the way He did, and what His mission was. He used the Scriptures as a dependable standard of truth. Jesus said the Scriptures given by God are always true: "Your word is truth" (John 17:17).

By emulating the ways of Jesus and being obedient to Him, we show the kind of disciplined love that equals the devotion Rizpah had for her two sons, but our devotion yields a far greater reward. The test of our obedience is our willingness to hear the words of Jesus and then to act on them. James

1:21-25 outlines it this way:

> Therefore, get rid of all moral filth and the evil that is so prevalent, and humbly accept the word planted in you, which can save you.
> 
> Do not merely listen to the word, and so deceive yourselves. Do what it says. Anyone who listens to the word but does not do what it says is like a man who looks at his face in a mirror, and after looking at himself, goes away and immediately forgets what he looks like. But the man who looks intently into the perfect law that gives freedom, and continues to do this, not forgetting what he has heard, but doing it—he will be blessed in what he does.

James points out that we are to approach our study of the life and teachings of Jesus in pureness and meekness and with a sense of being in training to become doers of His bidding. This, then, is the basis of the Jesus Effect as it applies to love: Jesus is a manifestation of love itself, and by serving Him, we are filling our lives with love. To know Jesus is to know love.

## Chapter Three

# Endurance

George Meegan spent seven years walking 19,017 miles from the southernmost tip of South America to the northernmost tip of Alaska. He is listed in the *Guinness Book of World Records* for having completed, in 1977, the longest continuous walking trip. When interviewed about this amazing feat, Meegan said, "I never thought of it as two continents. I focused only on the mile immediately ahead of me. If I ever became discouraged, I'd remind myself that I had already walked thousands of miles, so one more mile would be easy. Finally, the walk was over."

To me, the important lesson found within

Meegan's story is his understanding that the key to endurance is to do what you can with what you have for just a little bit longer. People often give up too quickly when only a little more effort could have led them to victory.

Jesus taught that if people will have the faith to complete a project, they *will* finish it. All it takes is that little bit of extra effort and confidence. Christ said, "If you have faith as small as a mustard seed, you can say to this mountain, 'Move from here to there,' and it will move. Nothing will be impossible for you" (Matthew 17:20).

Now, that may seem like too small an element of faith to get anyone through to the end of a project; nevertheless, history has shown us countless times that just that little bit of extra faith in yourself and your work can give you the endurance to find victory.

Note some of these "mustard seed" factors that led people to great victories:

Roger Maris became baseball's all-time single season home-run champion by hitting just one more home run than Babe Ruth had hit in a single season.

Roger Bannister became the first person to break the four-minute mile in running. His speed of 3 minutes, 59.4 seconds was less than a 1-percent improvement over world-record-holder Gunder Haegg of Sweden, whose best time had been 4 minutes, 1.4 seconds.

When A. J. Foyt won the Indianapolis 500 in 1961, he was only five seconds faster than second-place winner Eddie Sacks, despite the fact that the race had lasted for more than three-and-a-half hours.

These examples—a few of many—show that just a small amount of extra endurance can mean the difference in success or failure. Let me share a more personal example with you. My father, L. Edward Hensley, determined when he was a very young boy that one day he would become a successful businessman. He determined this in spite of the fact that as a youngster he seemed to have everything going against him.

When his father developed tuberculosis, my father had to quit school after the eighth grade to support his parents and little sister. As my father picked cotton during the ninety-degree Tennessee summer, he watched cars drive by on a nearby road. There and then he made a vow to himself: he would endure whatever was necessary in order to gain an education and to secure a good occupation. He promised himself that somehow he would escape the cotton fields and one day drive down that road in a fancy car of his own.

At age fifteen my father traveled north to Detroit, where he found work running a candy-and-newspaper stand in a bank by day. Each evening he attended trade school, where he finished his high-school diploma as well as learned how to be an optician. At age seventeen he enlisted in the U.S. Navy and did sea duty in Central and South America during the last months of World War II. At eighteen he married my mother, and at twenty they bought their first home. I was born later that year.

My father started his own optical business, but it

was not a success. He refused to give up, however. He next formed a partnership with two other opticians, but that company went bankrupt. Despite all this, he refused to give up his dream of becoming successful in business. He learned from each of his mistakes and became wiser the next time out.

Although he had to drive a cab at night to help support us, as well as work in someone else's optical grinding lab as a regular job, he made time to read books, attend conventions, and carefully follow the trade magazines. During the late 1950s he concentrated his studies on a newly developed product called "contact lenses." Most other opticians thought they were a gimmick item, something that would be forgotten within two or three years. But not my father.

He predicted a time when millions of people would be wearers of contact lenses. He formed the Phoenix Contact Lens Company on borrowed money and, in time, became so successful that he was able to buy out all of his silent partners. He renamed the business the Hensley Contact Lens Company. Later, he formed a subsidiary optical lens business and then a prosthetic eye laboratory. He bought his own building and hired several employees to work for him.

After his businesses were going well, he bought a Lincoln Continental automobile. He took my mother, brother, sister, and me on a trip to Camden, Tennessee, where he had lived as a boy and had picked cotton. As we drove down the road near the cotton fields, my father smiled and said, "At last! At last!" It was a personal triumph made possible by personal endurance and undaunted persistence.

If you look for one common factor in the lives of successful people, you will find endurance—the endurance to see something through to the end no matter how overwhelming the odds may seem or how great the task may be.

Truly, endurance is the only common denominator that you will find in great leaders. For example, you cannot say that all great leaders are physically attractive. For every handsome John F. Kennedy, you will find a dozen homely Abe Lincolns, bald Winston Churchills, and plain Golda Meirs. Nor can you point to wealth. Andrew Carnegie arrived in America as a penniless immigrant, Benjamin Franklin began as a printer's assistant, and Ronald Reagan once worked as a five-dollar-per-week radio announcer in Iowa.

The only quality that great leaders and successful people of all walks of life have in common, other than the basic motivation they share to *become* successful, is their endurance. The Bible tells of Joseph, who dreamed of becoming greater than all his brothers. He was subsequently sold into slavery, put into prison, released from prison to become a bond servant, framed by Potiphar's wife and returned to prison, and then finally vindicated and made the second most powerful man in Egypt. He faced one setback after another, but he never forgot his original dream of success. After enduring hardship and delay, he reached his goal.

## A quality of endurance

Jesus preached a message of endurance for His

followers. He said, "All men will hate you because of me, but he who stands firm to the end will be saved" (Mark 13:13).

Jesus gave a living example of endurance. He endured the rigors of the wilderness fast and still resisted the temptations of Satan. He endured the scourging of the whip and the tearing of the thorns and the piercing of the nails—and still fulfilled His mission.

Christ knew that living the Christian life would not be easy for His converts. He warned about the difficulty in a story He told about a farmer who randomly threw seeds all over his property. The seed that fell on stony ground developed no roots and, consequently, it dried up in the sun and died. The seed that fell among the thorns was choked out and was never able to grow. But the seed that fell on rich, well-cultivated soil grew to be strong plants that yielded a tremendous harvest.

Christ explained that Christians were often like the farmer's seed. Those who hear the word of God but never take it to heart are like seed on stony ground; they wither and fall prey to Satan. Others who hear the word but never allow it to change their lives are like seed living among thorns; in time, they are choked out by sin. The people who hear the word and live by it, no matter what sort of endurance that calls for, are like the seed that fell on good soil; they grow in spiritual grace, live by the training they are rooted in, and, in time, yield great fruits of ministry.

Thus, a lack of endurance can lead to failure in the Christian life. Jesus said that people who are like seed on stony ground "have no root in themselves, and so *endure but for a time*: afterward, when affliction or persecution ariseth for the word's sake, immediately they are offended" (Mark 4:17, KJV, emphasis supplied).

By setting these examples in word and deed, Jesus taught us what real endurance is. The apostle Paul, who himself endured beatings and imprisonment for the cause of Christ, wrote many messages to Timothy, telling him to become a person who can endure hardships for the Lord's sake. Said Paul, "Endure hardship with us like a good soldier of Christ Jesus" (2 Timothy 2:3). He also told Timothy to "endure hardship" (2 Timothy 4:5) and not let it be a hindrance to his work as an evangelist.

We see, then, that the Jesus Effect as it applies to endurance is this: to know *what* your mission for God is and to be so convinced that it is worthy of achievement that no amount of criticism or personal weakness will ever keep you from reaching that goal.

Chapter
# Four

# Boldness

During the 1960s I watched racial tension escalate on my college campus. One day a number of black students blocked the entrance to the science facility. Each of these students, clenched fist raised in the air, chanted, "Say it loud: I'm black and I'm proud." Some carried baseball bats; others held knives.

Facing them was a group of white students. Some held rocks; one boy held a handle of an automobile jack. They jeered and taunted the black students, threatening to rush en masse past the blacks to force open the doors. The young white men began to chant, "Say it right: It's best to be white."

As I stood there watching, four cars of city police officers and campus security guards pulled up. Officers carrying nightsticks and bullhorns moved between the groups of protesters and ordered them to disperse or face arrest. Within fifteen minutes access to the science building was restored, and the potential rioters were disbanded, each group threatening, however, to return if their demands weren't met.

I couldn't approve of the action taken by either of the two groups. The black students had broken the law by denying other students access to a public building (something they themselves had had to face during the 1950s). The white students were wrong to assume that violence and force were the only ways to resolve the conflict. Even though I disagreed with the actions of both groups, one thing made a lasting impression on me. Both sides were willing to air their opinions publicly *and* to take a stand for them. Right or wrong, these people had the boldness to stand up for their beliefs.

Would to God that today's Christians would have such a boldness to share their faith and to proclaim their redeemed status. More than ever, we need to have a say-so Christianity alive in our land. Psalm 107:2, KJV, admonishes, "Let the redeemed of the Lord say so."

Taking a stand for the cause of Christ has never been easy. The Bible tells us of Stephen, Peter, Paul, and others who were killed because of their faith. John was exiled to the Isle of Patmos. Barnabas was whipped and imprisoned. Christianity and physical persecution seemed to have been synonymous in the early church.

Though today in America we enjoy religious freedom, it is still difficult to be bold for the Lord. When I was in college, I did not join a fraternity because I felt my testimony would be hampered by associating with students who sponsored beer parties, hung lewd posters on the walls of their study rooms, and planned humiliating (often dangerous) initiations for new members. Naturally, because of my decision, I forfeited the chance to make a lot of new friends. Even worse, I was ridiculed for not joining the fun, for not being a team player, and for not becoming part of the "Now Generation."

Later, in the military, because I didn't use off-color language, didn't smoke, didn't drink beer, didn't play cards and gamble, and didn't go to town each payday in search of "skirts," I was frequently the object of crude jokes or cutting remarks. It would have been so much easier just to make a few concessions and become "one of the guys."

The business world has not proven to be any different. One of my clients quit using my consulting services because I politely asked him in private if he would refrain from swearing whenever we talked. Another former client told me that he didn't feel comfortable going to lunch with me after business meetings because I never ordered a cocktail.

Now, before you start feeling sorry for my "outcast" situation, let me assure you that the advantages of living my testimony have far outweighed any needling I've had to endure over the years. As my grandmother used to tell me, "Cream rises to the top."

She was right. For every twenty people who may want to mock your disciplined walk and Christian stand, there will be at least one person who will feel the same way you do. That one person will rise to the top, and you will be able to find him or her if you really look.

I am acquainted with a lot of people. I truly enjoy being with most of them—my neighbors, my business colleagues, my clients, my dentist, my doctor, my former professors. On assessment, however, I have to admit that I have only a dozen truly close friends; and of that number, I have only four men whom I would call "a friend who sticks closer than a brother" (Proverbs 18:24). (For a fact, one of these four men happens to *be* my brother.)

I wouldn't trade my friendships with these men for anything. No matter how difficult times may ever be for me, I can always turn to these *buddies* of mine and find a word of encouragement or advice. I'm flattered to think that they feel the same way about me. When I am frequently tempted to stray from the disciplines of my faith (for like Paul, I, too, feel as though I have to "die daily" for my beliefs), I think of these outstanding friends of mine, and I use them as role models. If they can hold fast, so can I.

In everything about them—their moral character, their family leadership, their business ethics, their gentlemanly speech, their work in the church—they give evidence of a love for Christ and a loyalty of His teachings. If, like the prophet of old, I am ever inclined to think I am the only one who has not bent a knee in honor of Baal, I have these friends to keep things in perspective. I am not alone. Other people also practice a say-so Christianity.

## A quiet boldness

Jesus demonstrated two kinds of boldness. He used quiet boldness when facing His adversaries, without flamboyantly defending Himself or His actions. This was best demonstrated by the silence when He stood before the Roman procurators after being accused of heresy, rebellion, and blasphemy. He would not recant His earlier claims to being the Messiah, but neither would He match evil for evil by heaping scorn on His accusers. He, of course, also showed an *active boldness* for the cause of righteousness. We can find many examples, ranging from His youthful debate with the elders to driving the money-changers from the temple courtyard. As Christians, we need to emulate Christ in both of these expressions of boldness.

Quiet boldness can have tremendous impact on people who are non-Christians, for it demonstrates a special inner confidence everyone desires yet few possess.

During the war in Vietnam, I served in the 184th Military Police Company of the United States Army. My assignment was to work as a chaplain's assistant. While on base in Long Binh, I did secretarial duties for the chaplain. However, when the chaplain visited troops in the jungle, I became the chaplain's bodyguard (chaplains, like medics, do not bear arms, even in a combat zone).

Sometimes I looked like Pancho Villa, with my bandoleers criss-crossed over my chest, a .45-caliber pistol holstered on my hip, a bayonet in a scabbard attached to my belt, and an M-16 rifle in my hands. One day the chaplain looked at me and said, "Just take the rifle and a couple of extra magazines of shells, Hensley. If we run into worse trouble than that can handle, it's going to be curtains for us anyway." With that, he laughed. And when I thought about his logic, so did I. Who did I think I was? John Wayne? G.I. Joe? Get real, Hensley!

I enjoyed working with that chaplain. His name was Wayne King. He was a major, originally a Baptist preacher from Texas, on his second tour of duty in Vietnam. In 1968 he had served with the First Cavalry Division near the DMZ (demilitarized zone), and now in 1971 he was back and assigned to the military police. The two things I remember most about Chaplain King are his incredible sense of humor (his sermons were a joy to hear) and his constant sense of inner peace. I never once saw an expression of panic or fear cross his face, even in the most desperate combat situations.

I wasn't the only person who sensed this quiet boldness in Chaplain King. Once, in the middle of the dry season, I went with the chaplain to visit a unit on full alert. Reports of Viet Cong activity in the area indicated that a strike against the American firebase might take place that very day.

Everyone was tense. Lookouts and scouts were patrolling the perimeter and calling back reports on their radios. Enlisted men were armed and in positions behind sandbags and in bunkers. Officers were checking and rechecking supplies and equipment. The heat was insufferable, and the tension was putting tremendous strain on everyone.

Amidst all this, Chaplain King was casually strolling from one bunker to the next in order to chat with the men. He would hand each guy a stick of gum and then say, "Any of you guys named Joshua?" The soldiers would shake their heads and say No. "Hmmm," the chaplain would muse. "Well, somebody around here sure seems to be holding the sun up there on full blast."

The men would smile at this, and then the chaplain would launch into some silly yarn about something funny that had supposedly happened during his days of playing high-school football or perhaps during his years as a young preacher in east Texas. (A favorite one was the story he would tell about when one of his parishioners, a cattle baron, pulled a gun on him the day he tried to preach about the ninety and nine *sheep*.)

Chaplain King would end his little visits by reading a couple of verses from the Bible. A frequent one he used was 2 Timothy 1:7, "God did not give us a spirit of timidity, but a spirit of power, of love, and of self-discipline." He then would pray briefly with the men and move on.

Everyone always felt better after one of these visits with the chaplain. The men loved him. From the faded "1st Cav" patch on his left shoulder, the men knew that the chaplain had seen his share of combat. This was no wimpy preacher who came by to pat the boys on the back and say, "Keep the faith, fellows," only to retreat to the rear. Nope, this chaplain was the real goods. He walked his talk, and he did it with a quiet boldness that inspired other men.

On that particular day of the impending attack, the chaplain and I entered a bunker where only one man was on duty. He seemed incredibly agitated. The chaplain and I both recognized the signs of a man who had never been in a battle before. The man was sweating so profusely that his entire uniform had turned a dark-greenish-black. The chaplain told him to sit down and relax a minute. The chaplain then moved up near the open front of the bunker and took over the man's lookout duties.

The soldier's hands were shaking. He looked ill. He removed his helmet and wiped his forearm across his forehead. Slowly, not making any sudden moves, he inched up near Chaplain King.

"You don't sweat like the rest of us," he said.

"I sweat," said the chaplain, wiping his forehead to emphasize the point.

"Uh-uh. Not like us," insisted the soldier. "You . . . well . . . you perspire 'cause it's hot. But you don't sweat. You never get pale and pasty-faced like we do. You don't swim in sweat like the rest of us. And it's 'cause you ain't scared. I don't understand that. Why ain't you scared, Major?"

The chaplain kept his eyes straight ahead, scanning the area beyond the bunker.

"Why ain't you scared?" demanded the soldier, moving closer to the chaplain. "How come you ain't cussing and crying and . . . and . . . well, *sweatin'* like the rest of us? You think them Viet Cong wouldn't kill you as quick as they'd kill me? Huh? I'm talking to you, sir. Answer me."

The chaplain kept his eyes forward. "They're going to kill me a lot sooner if you don't keep your voice down. Take a sip out of your canteen and get a hold of yourself."

"It's empty," said the soldier. "Not a drop left. See?"

He waved the empty container.

"Here," said the chaplain, keeping his eyes on the area outside, but reaching backward to pull his canteen from his web belt. "Have some of mine. It's warm though."

The soldier turned on his back, slid down into the bunker a bit, then lifted the canteen. He gulped hard twice, then caught himself. He could have finished the entire can. Instead, he carefully recapped it and handed it back.

"Keep it," said the chaplain, without looking. "Give me your empty one. I can wait."

The soldier was surprised. "You sure, Major?" he asked. "Don't seem right."

"Forget it," said Chaplain King. He reached blindly for the empty canteen, caught it, and put it into his belt pouch. His eyes never left the perimeter in front of the bunker.

"I swear I can't understand it," said the soldier, now somewhat calmer. "You don't sweat, you don't drink water, you don't cuss. A man's gotta release tension somehow out here. But you—you ain't human, Chaplain."

The chaplain averted his eyes for an instant and stole a glance at me. He then turned toward the other soldier.

"I'm human," he said flatly. "All too human. That's the trouble. I can control the spirit. It's the human body I have trouble with. This little skirmish in the jungle today won't be anything compared to *that* war. I'm just glad the Good Lord saw fit to give me a secret weapon."

Chaplain King's eyes returned to the perimeter. He squinted for a sharper view, checking to see if he had missed anything in his momentary distraction.

"Spirit?" said the soldier. "You mean you believe in spirits and stuff?"

He inched his way back to the edge of the bunker's viewing area. "What'd ya mean about the secret weapon? You get something the rest of us ain't been issued yet?"

The chaplain couldn't help but smile. "I've never thought of it that way," he responded in an even voice, "but, yeah, I guess you could say that."

"How'd you get it?" asked the soldier.

"Blood."

The soldier's eyes widened. "Killed a man? You mean, you killed a man?"

"I didn't kill him," answered Chaplain King. "He died in my place. It was his own free choice."

"Where'd it happen? Ben Hoa? DaNang? Phu Loi? Hey—was it that chopper crash you were in last month at Firebase Bravo?"

"No," said the chaplain. "Not last month. This happened about two thousand years ago."

The soldier stared at Chaplain King for a moment. Then he slowly pulled out the canteen of water. "You ever had sunstroke before?" he asked.

The chaplain kept his eyes fixed straight ahead.

"I'm fine," he said, a slight grin forming on his face. "Don't they celebrate Easter or Christmas where you come from, troop?"

"Huh?"

"I was talking about Christ," explained Chaplain King. "When He came to earth as an infant, He gave us hope for eternal life. That's why we still celebrate Christmas. Later, when He died on the cross, His blood was a sacrifice for all people's sins. He made it possible for us to live eternally." He paused a second, then added, "And that's why I don't sweat, son. Whether I make it through this battle today or I don't, sometime I'm going to die. You are too. But the difference between you and me is, I'm ready to die. You aren't. And that's what makes you so uneasy about facing battle."

"I don't want to die," the soldier admitted, as he lowered his head.

"Then don't," suggested the chaplain.

The man's head jerked up. "What?"

"If you are afraid to die, then don't die," Chaplain King repeated. "You can exist with Christ in paradise if you accept Him now as your Saviour. You'll go on living, and in a far better place than here on earth."

"I never grew up in no church," said the man.

"I'm not talking about church," the chaplain interrupted. He signaled for me to take his place as lookout. I moved into position. "I'm talking about faith, son. I have it and I can share it with you."

The chaplain pulled out his Bible and outlined the plan of redemption to the young soldier. The man was eager to hear and learn how he could be like Chaplain King. They talked and prayed together for a long time, and then the young man accepted Christ as His Saviour. Almost immediately he looked as if a great weight had been lifted from him.

As the chaplain and I started to leave the bunker a few minutes later, the new convert called to Chaplain King. "Wait a minute, Chaplain," he said. He pulled the half-full canteen from his web gear and tossed it to the chaplain. "Here's yours back. I won't need it. Give me my empty one. I don't think I'll be sweating as hard as I was before."

## The active boldness

The quiet boldness Chaplain King possessed earned him the respect and trust of the men around him. The more the other officers and enlisted men were around him, the more they wanted to have what he had—that inner peace and total confidence, that obvious assurance that all was well in his life.

Often, Chaplain King was able to pass along this quiet boldness to others. This was an excellent example of how the Jesus Effect relates to boldness. Christ Himself said, "Peace I leave with you; my peace I give you. I do not give to you as the world gives. Do not let your hearts be troubled and do not be afraid" (John 14:27). Jesus had a quiet boldness, and He showed others how they could have it too.

Other situations, however, may require a more active boldness. Corrie ten Boom tells in her book *The Hiding Place* of having to defy the orders of the occupying German army. Her decision to risk her life and property in order to hide Jews resulted in being interned in a concentration camp, where her sister died in her arms. Many years later, as an old woman, Corrie frequently said that she never regretted her decisions or actions and that, for a fact, she would repeat them if she had the opportunity. It was "the right thing to do as a Christian," she insisted.

When David Wilkerson took the gospel to inner-city gang members, he was threatened, sworn at, and attacked. He refused to give up, however. His dedication eventually led to the conversion of gang leader Nicki Cruz, who later entered full-time Christian service. Cruz, in turn, emulated Wilkerson's boldness by also developing ministries to street kids, runaways, addicts, and prostitutes.

When Los Angeles Dodger pitcher Orel Hershiser sang the Doxology on Johnny Carson's "Tonight Show," it took active boldness. When evangelist Billy Graham preached the gospel in Russia, it took active boldness. When Jimmy Carter continued to teach a Sunday School class even during his presidency, it took active boldness.

People like these folks have a say-so Christianity. They are applying the Jesus Effect to active boldness and are sharing the joy of their faith. Christ taught, " 'No one lights a lamp and puts it in a place where it will be hidden, or under a bowl. Instead, he puts it on its stand, so that those who come in may see the light.' " " 'If your whole body is full of light, and no part of it dark, it will be completely lighted, as when the light of a lamp shines on you' " (Luke 11:33, 36).

Jesus lived by His own mandates. He was not afraid to stand before the lawyers and Pharisees and Sadducees to denounce their sins. " 'And you experts in the law, woe to you' " (Luke 11:46). " 'Now then, you Pharisees clean the outside of the cup and dish, but inside you are full of greed and wickedness' " (Luke 11:39).

Christ cast out the demons. He faced Satan in the wilderness. He debated the Sanhedrin. He drove the money-changers out of the temple. When it called for an act of righteous boldness, Christ never hesitated. His chief weapon of combat was Scripture. He quoted Old Testament writings to the priests and scribes, and He shunned Satan's temptations by referring to Scripture passages.

## Say-so Christianity

If we want to rise from so-so Christianity to say-so Christianity, we need to have both the quiet and the active boldness that Christ patterned while on earth. As we have seen in this chapter, modern Christians can display boldness for the cause of Christ in various ways. When we are armed with "the full armor of God" (Ephesians 6:13) we can put fears aside.

God—who can do all things—has chosen to allow men and women to help carry out His work on earth. It is our obligation to do this work. We must not shirk or wince. Psalm 68:35 says, "The God of Israel gives power and strength to His people." Jesus used this strength and power to be bold in the face of adversity. We can use this same power and strength to follow His pattern of boldness.

## Chapter Five

# Humility

While human beings were building the *Titanic*, God was building the iceberg. While we were creating the Tower of Babel, God was creating new languages. While we were designing an airplane, God was designing birds. While we were channeling electricity, God was channeling lightning.

Our greatest efforts have always been utterly puny when measured alongside God's wonderments. Mark Twain was correct when he noted, "Man is the only animal that blushes. Or needs to." We have so much to be humble about. Even our personal righteousness is nothing more than "filthy rags" apart from the cleansing of Christ's blood on our behalf.

Ironically, it is often people of great prestige and status who are most aware of the awesomeness of God and the puniness of human beings. King David, Israel's mightiest military leader and most astute statesman, saw himself as merely a speck on life's continuum. He fell to the ground and cried aloud to God, "What is man that you are mindful of him?" (Psalm 8:4). David had learned the value of a humble heart.

But what *are* the lessons of humility? Jesus Himself bent before each of His disciples and washed their feet, then dried them with the towel wrapped around His waist. Peter, in his zeal to show love for Christ, refused to let Jesus wash his feet. But Jesus insisted; He had a lesson to teach Peter.

It had been a requirement in the days of Moses that when the priests approached the holy tabernacle, they first washed their hands and feet (see Exodus 30:17-21). Failure to complete this symbolic cleansing resulted in death.

When Jesus came to earth, there no longer was a need for a tabernacle. God was there, in the flesh, among humanity. The holiness of the tabernacle had symbolized the holiness of Jesus. It was still appropriate to approach this holiness in a state of cleanliness. Yet, note the difference: the Holy One was, Himself, assisting the unclean worshipers to cleanse themselves.

"I have set you an example," Jesus explained, "that you should do as I have done for you" (John 13:15).

And what had He done? Several things. He had used humility rather than pride to demonstrate love and devotion to His followers. He had brought eleven people to a state of spiritual cleanliness. He had shown devotion to His heavenly Father by putting Himself in the role of a servant, ready to do His Father's will.

If the disciples could emulate this humility in their actions toward one another, they would always remain a team (see John 13:14). If they could show humility in serving others in the world, they would fulfill their commission from Christ (see John 13:16).

Christ demonstrated that one of the greatest aspects of leadership is the willingness to be a servant. "If any man desire to be first," explained Jesus, "the same shall be last and servant of all."

## Understanding the concept

A story is told of a pompous sergeant who ordered a private to move a heavy log. The private pulled and tugged and struggled, but he could not carry the log by himself. After a time a gentleman wearing an expensive cape and new black boots rode by on a white stallion.

"Shouldn't you help this man move the log?" the gentleman asked the sergeant.

"Out of the question," roared the sergeant. "I'm a sergeant. I'll not dirty my hands in common work with a mere private!"

Hearing this, the gentleman dismounted his horse. He grabbed one end of the log and lifted it. The private grabbed the other end, and together they carried it to the defense barrier being prepared.

"Thank you," said the private. "I appreciate your help. Tell me, sir, what is your name?"

The gentleman threw back his cape and revealed the uniform of a general.

"Washington," said the gentleman. "George Washington." And with that a great cheer rose from the nearby group of enlisted men.

This lesson in leadership through humility has been demonstrated time and again. Once, when the troops of Alexander the Great had gone two days without water, Alexander emptied the cup of water that had been saved for him. As he poured it into the sand he announced loudly, "I will drink after my army drinks, and not before." His men cheered ecstatically.

General Robert E. Lee spent many hours meeting the men in his command. He took no rations or blankets for himself beyond what was given to every other soldier in his outfit. He became so beloved, his troops once refused to go into battle until Lee rode to the safety of the rear of the column.

Field Marshal Erwin Rommel flew with his reconnaissance pilots over enemy territory prior to battles during the North African campaign. He never asked anything of his men that he wasn't willing to do himself. Because of the loyalty and dedication of his troops, Rommel was able to hold back British and American forces even after his fuel and ammunition supplies were virtually exhausted. If Rommel stayed in the field, so did his men.

When John F. Kennedy's PT boat was cut in

half and sunk by a Japanese warship, young Kennedy took a turn at swimming each night in the channel between the islands where he and his men had been washed ashore. Kennedy bobbed, floated, and treaded water for hours, carrying flashlights he hoped to use to flag down any passing U.S. ship. He did this despite pulled back muscles and three cracked ribs. Such dedication and willingness to serve later garnered him the Navy Cross and a promotion. Each man in his command turned in a report of the selfless gallantry of their lieutenant.

Mother Teresa has spent her adult life caring for the homeless of India. She seeks no personal recognition nor any special rewards. Upon receiving the Nobel Prize, she used the money to buy supplies for the clinics she directs. Major news magazines have featured her face on their covers, yet she has gone about her days laboring as a nurse, bookkeeper, cook, waitress, janitor, and prayer partner. Her consistent dedication to caring for the poor and needy has resulted in the saving of thousands of lives.

## The common factor

If we looked for a common denominator that links people as diverse as Mother Teresa and General Robert E. Lee, we would find one similarity. Each of these persons was completely dedicated to a cause that merited his or her total commitment. No sacrifice was too great, no challenge was too difficult, no work was too demanding or too demeaning. It was the *noble cause* in each instance that counted, not the fame or obscurity of the workers.

This is exactly the sort of total dedication to the cause of salvation that Jesus revealed throughout His ministry. "Not my will, Father, but thine," was His humble prayer.

When Christians emulate the behavior of Christ, they accomplish remarkable things. One person who proved this to me was Oren Whitman, a man who served for twenty-eight years as the janitor of First Baptist Church of Bay City, Michigan, where I grew up. I remember going to the funeral parlor the day after Brother Whitman died. The room was filled with dozens of vases of flowers, and visitors were standing shoulder to shoulder. It took me thirty minutes to work my way up to the casket to offer my condolences to the widow.

I shook hands with Mrs. Whitman and said, "You and your children have my sympathy. Your husband was a wonderful Christian and a fine gentleman. I always enjoyed talking to him whenever I came to the church. He was also an excellent building janitor."

Mrs. Whitman's soft smile suddenly became strained.

"Oh, no," she corrected. "I'm afraid you're wrong about that. My husband never considered himself a mere building janitor. He had a far greater responsibility than that. He told me often that he was the official custodian of God's own house. That's why he was such a fanatic about everything he did. He was working directly for God. Only his best effort would be good enough."

I was captivated by this. As I looked around the

room, I saw nearly three hundred people who had been touched by Oren Whitman's excellent work. Here were people who had been married in our church, who had worshiped in our church, who had attended funerals in our church, who had been baptized in our church. In some way, all of their lives had been impacted by our church, and it had been Brother Whitman who had, for twenty-eight years, seen to it that the church was always well maintained and ready to use. His humble attitude and total dedication to serving God had been a positive force at our church for nearly three decades. He had taken the admonition, "Whatsoever thou doest, do so unto the Lord" as his personal call to excellence. He did his work quietly, faithfully, and humbly—and the results were impressive.

Oren Whitman, like Christ Himself, looked beyond the mundane tasks at hand and kept an eye on the bigger picture: the noble cause. I am sure that to Mr. Whitman it was a fair exchange. Jesus had gone to heaven to prepare a home for Oren Whitman (see John 14:1-3), so, meanwhile, Oren Whitman was taking good care of Christ's church.

## The humility of Christ

In all that He did, Jesus showed humility. He walked with rulers and commoners. He ate with the righteous and the unrighteous. He did not condemn the harlot but, instead, challenged her to begin a new life. He welcomed the little children to come to Him. He obeyed the request of His mother and provided wine for the wedding feast. He rejected Satan's offers of leadership over earthly kingdoms.

Jesus was not a braggart. When He healed the blind man at Bethsaida (see Mark 8:26), He instructed him, "Don't go into the village." Jesus sought no publicity. He had restored the man's sight and his soul, and that was enough. Similarly, when Jesus had convinced His disciples of His identity and missions, He ordered them not to brag about it to other people (see Mark 8:30).

Jesus was totally dedicated to His mission. It was the cause that mattered, not His personal glory. One day He would again sit at the right hand of the Father, but while on earth the commitment to the work at hand was all that mattered.

In using the Jesus Effect as it applies to humility, we, too, should be willing to put aside personal vanities and, instead, emulate the Master who taught us, through His walk, to be humble.

The apostle Peter was quick-tempered, rowdy, and loud. After associating with Jesus, Peter's character changed. He became tolerant, forgiving, and gracious. Using Christ as his example, Peter taught his fellow Christians, "Clothe yourselves with humility toward one another, because, 'God opposes the proud, but gives grace to the humble.' Humble yourselves, therefore, under God's mighty hand, that he may lift you up in due time" (1 Peter 5:5, 6).

God's hand is still mighty and so are His deeds; and the greatest of His deeds is the creation of His plan of salvation. Knowing that it is available to us for "the asking" should humble us all.

## Chapter Six

# Forgiveness

Here is a question I want you to read twice; then, close this page on your thumb and sit for a few minutes, thinking carefully about the answer:

Would Jesus be a hard person to work for?

I was asked this same question by a friend of mine one day when we were having lunch together. My friend was having some problems with two employees in his office. One new secretary couldn't seem to type a memo or letter without having at least two spelling errors on each page. A sales rep failed to follow up on all of the client leads my friend was assigning to him.

In both cases my friend had counseled these two people, had taught them ways to do better work, and had explained the benefits for the company and for the employees of "a job well done." Nevertheless, the employees continued to do substandard work.

"I want my office to do excellent work for our parent company," said my friend, "yet in order to get things accomplished the right way, I wind up acting like a tyrant. Sometimes I get so frustrated over slipshod work turned in that I completely lose my patience and start yelling. I know that's no way for a Christian to behave. I just keep wondering how Jesus would have handled this situation. Do you think He would be a hard person to work for?"

"The situation at your office is mild compared to the management problems Jesus faced," I answered. "Your secretary Cindy can't spell. What's that when compared to working with a guy like Judas who's plotting behind your back to have you killed? Your salesman Ted won't expand his customer base. What's that compared to having a guy like Peter traveling with you, knowing he may pull out a sword and try to kill anyone who disagrees with you?"

My friend smiled. "OK, so maybe my problems aren't that extreme. But they're still frustrating. How can I be a patient and gracious Christian, yet still produce good work for my company? It's tough being a manager when people don't live up to your expectations."

"I'm sure Jesus would agree with you on that point," I said. "Christ spent more than three years teaching His disciples, advising them, counseling them, empowering them, and then they *still* let Him down in the end. Jesus revived Peter's mother-in-law, yet Peter later denied three times that he even knew Jesus. Jesus had the disciples distribute the food when His miracle enabled 5,000 people to be fed, yet these same disciples couldn't even stay awake long enough to pray with Jesus in the garden at Gethsemane. Jesus predicted that He would rise from the dead—and He did!—but Thomas wouldn't believe Him until he touched His nail and spear wounds."

I paused a moment to allow all of this to sink in on my friend. After a while, my friend pressed an earlier point of his.

"You're only underscoring what I was saying before. It's hard to be a boss when people you work with let you down. And I'll agree with you that my management problems seem petty when compared to what Jesus had to deal with. Still . . . there's one big difference here."

"And what's that?" I asked.

"The *results*," he answered. "Despite the failures of the people who worked with Him, Jesus still managed to build a team of workers who reached the goals He had set. They established churches, they preached the gospel all over the world, they discipled younger men to carry on after them, they wrote the books of the New Testament—they achieved great things in spite of their failures. And that's the big difference. *My* workers aren't achieving anything. I could be more tolerant of their shortcomings if I could just see some overall progress. But I don't see it, and that makes me discouraged and angry. I need to see some success."

"You can't give up," I said. "Training and encouraging people are never-ending processes. But I think Jesus used two approaches that you haven't picked up on yet. That's probably why His people succeeded whereas yours haven't."

"Two approaches? *What* two approaches? I'm willing to try anything at this point."

I explained, "If you look closely at the life of Jesus in relationship to how He worked with His disciples, you'll see two things. First, rather than always trying to point out the mistakes His disciples made, He chose instead to catch them doing things right and to praise their efforts.

"For example, when Peter became the first disciple to recognize Jesus as the Son of God, the long-awaited Messiah, Jesus honored Peter's faith by saying that Peter was blessed with an insight revealed by the Father in heaven (see Matthew 16:17). This affirmation motivated Peter to want to live up to the high expectations Jesus had for him. It was positive reinforcement and positive motivation."

"But I do that with my employees," my friend insisted.

"No," I countered. "You think you do, but you really don't. Every time you call Cindy into your office and say, 'You've done it again, Cindy. You've made more spelling errors in this letter,' that sends a message to her that you're *expecting* her to fail. So, she does. You haven't motivated her to do otherwise."

"Well, how do you think Jesus would motivate

her?" my friend challenged me.

"I think that each time Cindy typed something that was flawless, He would call her in and say that such excellent work reflected well on the image of the company, and that Cindy seemed to be getting better each day at her work. This praise would make Cindy feel like a real part of the team, a valued colleague. It would inspire her to try to produce another flawless letter so that she could feel good again about herself and her work."

"OK, I can buy into that," said my friend. "At least, in theory. But what happens when she starts to slip again? Workers are never continually excellent in what they do. Sooner or later they start to get lax again."

"Unfortunately, that's true," I had to agree, "but that's where the second approach Jesus used comes in. Whenever His disciples would seem to grow weary or lose their momentum or have doubts about their work, Jesus would restate His goals and objectives for them and remind them of the worthiness of their mission."

I pulled a New Testament from my pocket and opened to Matthew 28:16-20.

"I want to read a passage to you that may amaze you," I told my friend. "After working three years with His disciples and then rising from the dead, Jesus still had to contend with men who were dubious about His power and identity. He dealt with this by ignoring their doubts and focusing instead on the restatement of the overall mission. Here, let me read this to you."

I read the following passage:

Then the eleven disciples went to Galilee, to the mountain where Jesus had told them to go. When they saw him, they worshiped him; but some doubted. Then Jesus came to them and said, "All authority in heaven and on earth has been given to me. Therefore go and make disciples of all nations, baptizing them in the name of the Father and of the Son and of the Holy Spirit, and teaching them to obey everything I have commanded you. And surely I will be with you always, to the very end of the age."

My friend nodded his understanding. "It never gets easy, does it? You just have to hang in there."

"That's what it comes down to," I agreed.

My friend was silent a moment; then he said, "Sometimes it's harder than other times, though. I think I could learn to work with and encourage Cindy. But I've got to tell you, Ted has been a major disappointment to me. I did everything for that guy. I leased a company car for him, I gave him a private office—I even turned over some of my own clients to him. And after all that, Ted still failed to hit his quota four out of seven months. I don't know if it's even worth the effort to try to salvage him or not."

"Why did you choose Ted for the job?" I asked.

"I felt he deserved it," said my friend. "He had been our top salesman for two years, *and* he had come up with several ideas for revamping our distribution process that had saved us thousands of dollars. I went to the top brass at our company and personally recommended that Ted be made my assistant district manager. I expected our sales to double overnight. I even promised those kind of results to the home office."

"What happened when you told this to Ted?"

"He told me I was expecting too much too soon. I was shocked by his defeatist attitude. This got us off to a bad start. Instead of pulling in tandem, we found ourselves looking over our shoulders, watching out for the other guy all the time. It may be my fault for overestimating Ted's capabilities."

I looked my friend square in the face. "You're a pretty good salesman, aren't you?"

"I've got one of the best sales records in our company," my friend responded proudly.

"OK, then, what if your reward for being a good salesman was to be given an order from an executive vice-president that you had to double your sales record next month and then keep things at that new level for the rest of the year?"

My friend flinched at the thought.

"What!" he said. "But that wouldn't be—"

"Reasonable?" I suggested. "Well, why then is it reasonable for you to demand that of Ted? You doubled his quota before he even had time to settle into his new job. And despite all that, he *still* reached that new double-quota level four times for you. And how did you reinforce his good work?"

My friend lowered his head. "Only by yelling at him when he missed his quota. No wonder he doesn't seem to enjoy his work any longer. I've just about ruined his motivation, haven't I?"

"You've put a damper on it," I concurred, "but I think Ted can regain his momentum if you'll just let him know you still have confidence in him."

"How? How can I show it?" he asked.

I flipped through the pages of my New Testament, talking as I did so.

"Let me show you how Jesus handled it," I said. "You remember how Christ told Peter that he was 'blessed' because he was the first disciple to proclaim Jesus to be the Son of God. Yet despite his faith, Peter later denied three times that he even knew Jesus. For all intents and purposes, Peter's ministry should have been finished right then. But Jesus did something to show Peter that He had forgiven him and that He still had confidence in him."

My friend leaned forward and watched closely as I located two verses in my Bible.

"Here in Luke 24:34 and again in 1 Corinthians 15:5, it says that after Jesus rose from the dead, He appeared to Simon Peter even before He met with the Emmaus disciples or the other ten apostles or any of the multitudes. He made meeting with Peter one of His top priorities. He reestablished their original bond and put Peter's failure behind them. In a very real sense, He recommissioned Peter to the work of the ministry."

My friend nodded. "And Peter preached a sermon at Pentecost that was dynamic enough to lead 3,000 people to salvation. What a turnaround. Amazing!"

"Yes, but not unbelievable," I said. "The power was available to Peter all along. It just took the forgiveness of Christ and the reaffirmation of His confidence to embolden Peter to use it."

"And you think that if Ted and I could forgive each other for our unrealistic expectations, we *both* could get back on the right track?"

"Ted needs to know you still believe in his abilities," I said. "You, however, need to know that Ted still believes in your abilities to be a good manager. You guys can accomplish both goals if you do what Jesus did with Peter—forgive, then reaffirm."

My friend grabbed the bill. "My treat," he said. "You've given me a lot to think about. Let's get together again tomorrow."

"Tomorrow?"

"Uh-huh. We'll meet here again, OK? And I'll bring Ted along. I want you to meet him. I'll let you be a witness to the way I'll be bragging about his good work. You know—reaffirming him."

"Good," I said. "And while you *reaffirm*, let's hope Ted can *forgive*."

"Forgive?" asked my friend.

"Forgive both of us," I joked, "for sticking him with the check."

Chapter

# Seven

# Communication

When I was studying for a doctorate in linguistics, I used to tutor foreign students who wanted to master English. I was forever emphasizing that they should expand their vocabulary by studying the dictionary and the thesaurus. "Try new words," I would insist. "Experiment with different phrases."

Then one day one of these students stormed into my office, glared at me with flinty eyes, and bellowed, "Much trouble! You get me much trouble!"

"What?" I said. "What do you mean, I got you into trouble? How?"

"Last month I ask you what to say to girl on first

date," he explained. "You told me to say to girl, 'You look like a vision.'"

"So? What's wrong with that?" I demanded.

"Nothing," he agreed, shaking his head. "But last night I have date with new girl. I use same phrase, only first I check thesaurus for new words like you always say to do."

"Uh-oh," I said, anticipating the problem. "What did you say instead of, 'You look like a vision'?"

"I said to new date, 'You look a sight.'"

Looking back on that incident, I can now smile over this young man's problem. He was saying something he felt would be perfectly appropriate to his date, yet it was completely misunderstood. It was an innocent mistake, yet a mistake that was costly to him.

Sometimes those of us who have been Christians for many years are guilty of similar mistakes. We assume that what we are saying to non-Christians will automatically be understood. But that's not true. As a result, our conversations sometimes sound something like this:

"Excuse me, friend, but are you saved?"

"Saved? Why should I be? I'm not even drowning."

"No, no, what I mean is, are you born again?"

"Me? Naw. I don't believe in that reincarnation stuff."

"No, you're misunderstanding me. I want to know if you've been washed in the blood of the Lamb."

"Oh, yuck! What kind of savage ritual is that? Get away from me, you maniac!"

We see then that no matter how honest our intentions are, if our language isn't appropriate, we won't succeed in our witnessing. I like the way The Living Bible interprets 1 Corinthians 14:8-11 regarding this problem:

> If the army bugler doesn't play the right notes, how will the soldiers know that they are being called to battle? In the same way, if you talk to a person in some language he doesn't understand, how will he know what you mean? You might as well be talking to an empty room.
>
> I suppose that there are hundreds of different languages and dialects in the world, and all are excellent for those who understand them, but to me they mean nothing. A person talking to me in one of these languages will be a stranger to me and I will be a stranger to him.

That passage of Scripture reminds me of a time years ago when I went out on a neighborhood visitation canvass with a church friend. My friend was eager to impress people that they needed to attend church and get right with God. His method of doing this needed some polish, however. When we knocked on the first door, an elderly gentleman answered.

"Have you heard the good news?" asked my companion.

"No," admitted the gentleman. "What is it?"

"You're on your way to hell!"

"Well, if that's the *good* news," the man responded, "I don't want to stick around for the *bad* news." And with that, he slammed the door in our faces.

Since that incident, my friend has learned to be more gracious and less shocking when meeting people for the first time. The Bible has many excellent suggestions on how to overcome the language barrier when trying to communicate with nonChristians. It's worthwhile to review these tips.

1. *Listen to the leading of the Holy Spirit so that you can be His spokesperson.*

When God communicated to young Samuel, he closed his mouth and opened his ears to listen carefully to what God wanted to share with him. His only speech was the submissive phrase, "Speak, for your servant is listening" (1 Samuel 3:10). David also inclined his ear to God and said, "I will listen to what God the Lord will say" (Psalm 85:8).

In communicating with lost souls, our role is similar to that of an interpreter at the United Nations. First, the interpreter hears the words of one speaker, and then she translates them into a language that listeners will understand. Through prayer and Bible study, we can hear the words of God, and then we can relay them to others. The important rule to remember, however, is to listen first, speak second.

2. *Communicate on the maturity level of the listener.*

Paul wrote in 1 Corinthians 13:11, "When I was a child, I talked like a child, I thought like a child, I reasoned like a child. When I became a man, I put childish ways behind me."

An experience during the Vietnam War taught me the importance of communicating on the appropriate level. One of my assignments as chaplain's assistant was to lead a weekly Bible study group in a military prison. Many of the prisoners who attended these sessions had never attended a home church, nor had they ever read the Bible. These men were in their twenties and thirties, yet they had never heard of David's battle with Goliath or Daniel's night in the lions' den or Christ's Sermon on the Mount. This amazed me, for I had been raised in a Christian home and had attended church all my life. I thought *everyone* knew about David and Daniel and Jesus. But that wasn't so. As such, even though I was teaching full-grown men, I had to teach them as babes in the Word.

It's important to be sensitive to another person's level of comprehension. We must be patient and share ourselves first and then our testimonies and then, eventually, our knowledge of the Scriptures. Pacing our presentations is crucial.

3. *Be open, honest, humble, and loving.*

We all hate to phone a store and hear an operator answer with the flat unemotional phrase, "Thank-you-for-calling-how-can-I-help-you?" Even though the words are polite, their monotone blandness reveals the fact that no personal commitment stands behind them. We don't really *believe* the operator is pleased we phoned that store.

Christian witnessing also needs sincerity and genuineness. You can mouth the right words, but if the personal belief is not evident, the listener will not be swayed. As Paul explained in 1 Corinthians 13:1, "If I speak in the tongues of men and of angels, but have not love, I am only a resounding gong or clanging cymbal."

After a man on our block sprained his ankle last spring, his neighbor spent a weekend afternoon tilling his garden spot for him. When the injured man tried to pay his neighbor, the neighbor said he wanted only one thing in payment: he would like the injured man to attend his church once. The man with the sprained ankle put his wallet away and said, "I've never had anyone be so concerned about me before. Yes, I'll go to church with you." The neighbor's work for his friend had made credible the concern expressed in his words.

4. *Use yourself as an example.*

A most effective form of television advertising is the personal endorsement. People parade before the camera to tell how XYZ shampoo made their hair fluffy and tangle free or how ABC dog food made their pets live an extra ten years. The TV viewer thinks, *Well, if it worked for them, it just might work for me. I'll try that product.*

Witnessing must be personalized too. You need to endorse your belief in Christianity by telling of how God has touched *your* life, how He has blessed *your* family, how He has changed *your* daily walk. Jesus told Nicodemus, "We speak of what we know, and we testify to what we have seen" (John 3:11).

All you need to do to communicate with people about the love of Christ is to learn it, live it, and lend it. People will read you before they will read the Bible. Knowing this, make sure you "carry your message" in all that you do.

When I look to Jesus as my example of how to communicate, I find that He chose to use parables, simple stories, easy-to-follow examples, and common objects (a mustard seed, a tower, a vineyard, a mountain) as visual aids and explanations. He reduced the complicated to what was practical and basic. His whole ministry was summarized in just two easy words: "Follow Me." Do I then dare to be more "sophisticated"? I would never presume to be so.

## Chapter Eight

# Prayer

Not long ago a man said to me, "I'd pray more if I believed it would do any good."

I responded, "You've got the cause and effect reversed. The fact is, you'd believe more if you would pray more."

Like this man, other people have come to me for counseling, despondent because God had not answered their prayers. As ridiculous as it may seem, I've discovered that many of them had never made their needs known to God in the first place. They assumed there was no need to pray "since God already knows the needs."

Indeed, God knows every need; but we were created for fellowship with Him, and prayer is an important aspect of that fellowship. David understood this. He pledged, "To you I pray" (Psalm 5:2); "evening and morning and at noon I will pray" (Psalm 55:17, NKJV). Daniel prayed three times each day, even when it meant risking his life to do so. John the Baptist spent years fasting and praying in preparation for his ministry.

No one would deny that these men were close to God. Nevertheless, they were unassuming and humble. Their conviction that their God was a caring, listening God prompted them to turn to Him with an intensity of prayer, believing that God would respond.

I heard a preacher once explain the basis of prayer power. "It's not the length of your prayers—how long they are; it's not the arithmetic of your prayers—how many there are; it's not the poetry of your prayers—how beautiful they are; it's not the volume of your prayers—how loud they are. It's the intensity. That's all that counts."

If we look for the ultimate example of prayer intensity, we will find it in the prayers of Jesus. He preceded all of His miracles—from the feeding of the 5,000 to the raising of Lazarus from the dead—with intense prayer. Nowhere is this better depicted than in Luke 22:41-44, when Jesus prayed that His human flesh would be strong enough to face and endure the crucifixion before Him: "He withdrew about a stone's throw beyond them, knelt down and prayed. . . . And being in anguish, he prayed more earnestly, and his sweat was like drops of blood falling to the ground."

Such earnest prayers do not go unanswered by a loving God. In that instance, Jesus was given the strength He requested: "An angel appeared to him and strengthened him" (verse 43).

It is important to note two things about Jesus' prayer in the garden. First, He made a personal request. He asked to be spared the pending death on the cross. In asking this, however, He qualified His request by saying that it should be denied if it was not in line with the will of God the Father. He yielded His will to the Father's.

When it was apparent that such a request could not be granted, the second thing Jesus prayed for was the strength *to do* the Father's will. This request was granted, illustrating an important fact about prayer. The power of prayer is God's empowering us to do what is right in *His* eyes.

God has a plan for our lives, which we are free to reject or submit to. Following God's leading brings us our greatest fulfillment, although yielding is seldom easy. We can emulate Jesus' prayer of submission this way: by making our needs and desires known to God, but asking that they be granted only if they are pleasing to Him.

I can personally vouch for the fact that yielding to God is difficult if it means accepting something other than what you have been praying for. In 1974 I suffered damage to the nerves near my left temple. The result was gross disfigurement of the entire left side of my face. My cheek sagged, my left eyelid would not close, my lips were twisted, half of my tongue was numb, and my forehead would not wrinkle on the left side. It was terrifying.

Instinctively, my prayers were for miraculous total recovery. I prayed fervently, but no healing came. After ten days in our city hospital, I was transferred to a large university research hospital. There, a young hospital chaplain stopped by for a visit. I told him I had prayed for my face to be healed, but there had been no improvement.

The chaplain opened his Bible and read me the Old Testament story of how Joseph was sold into slavery by his jealous brothers. By the story's end, Joseph had become the second most powerful man in Egypt. When he revealed his identity to his brothers, they were sure he would seek revenge. Instead, he forgave them. When they asked how he could be so magnanimous, he explained that God had used their evil to work His good.

"Now, you have a similar opportunity," the chaplain told me. "Life has dealt you a hard blow. Is your faith strong enough for you to stop praying for what *you* want and, instead, discover what good God can bring out of this?"

"But I'm paralyzed," I mumbled through numb and twisted lips.

"Just the one side of your face is," the chaplain countered. "Your legs, feet, hands, arms, and back work fine. So does your hearing, thinking, seeing, and sense of touch. Find out what God has in store for you. Yield to Him."

From then on I changed my prayer. I continued to ask for my face to be healed, but I also prayed that if healing was not part of God's will for me, then I requested the grace to accept my situation and to serve where He could use me.

To my total amazement, the paralysis turned out to be a complete blessing from God. I had to attend speech therapy class in order to learn how to speak clearly again. I was given tips on vocal projection, enunciation, delivery, and body language. Soon, I not only learned how to speak again, I developed into a public orator. Thanks to that training years ago, I now deliver more than eighty major speeches each year at colleges, universities, and corporations. I also teach a Sunday School class each week and make numerous guest appearances on radio and television stations. Had it not been for the paralysis, this phase of my career might never have opened itself to me.

In the years since 1974 I have regained the feeling and most of the motor movement of my forehead, nose, lips, and tongue. My eyelids and left cheek still show evidences of the original nerve damage, however. But I never think about it. If people ever ask me about it, I tell them, "It was something that seemed to start out bad, but through the power of prayer it wound up working to my good."

So, if you ever catch yourself saying, "I'd pray more if I thought it would do me any good," just change that to, "I'm praying *now*, Lord, so that I can discover what *is good* for my life!"

Chapter
# Nine

## Simplicity

These signs . . . are not . . . for laughs alone . . . The face they save . . . may be your own . . . Burma Shave."
When I was a kid, the interstate highway system was just starting to be built. Families drove on two-lane roads in a car that traveled less than fifty miles an hour. One company that tailored its advertising to this mode of travel was the Burma-Vita Corporation, makers of Burma Shave shaving cream and after-shave lotion.

As the family car would "zip" along at forty-five miles an hour, a series of five or six signs would come into view, each spaced 100 paces apart. When combined, the words formed a limerick or funny saying that would make the readers laugh (as well as remind them to buy Burma Shave products). For example, you might see, "The answer to . . . a maiden's prayer . . . is *not* a chin . . . of stubby hair . . . Burma Shave!" or perhaps, "His face was smooth . . . and cool as ice . . . and oh, Louise! . . . he smelled . . . so nice . . . Burma Shave!"

My brother and sister and I used to argue over whose turn it was to read aloud the next set of Burma Shave signs. My personal favorite was, "The Bearded Lady . . . tried a jar . . . and now . . . she is . . . a movie star . . . Burma Shave." My mother's favorite was, "If you should think . . . she likes those bristles . . . you try kissin' . . . a flower . . . with thistles . . . Burma Shave." Dad liked "Dewhiskered . . . kisses . . . defrosts . . . the . . . Mrs. . . . Burma Shave."

Sometimes the signs carried advice and warnings, such as, "Slow down, Pa . . . sakes alive . . . Ma just missed . . . signs four . . . and five . . . Burma Shave" and "Our blackened forest . . . smoulders yet . . . because . . . he flipped . . . a cigarette . . . Burma Shave."

The first Burma Shave signs appeared in 1927 on route 65 from Minneapolis to Red Wing, Minnesota. They were installed by the company's Ph.D.'s (post hole diggers). The signs were incredibly successful, and so they were spread nationwide. Even during the Great Depression, the Burma-Vita Corporation grossed nearly three million dollars a year. However, by 1963, cars were traveling at seventy miles an hour on freeways, and if a driver craned his neck to read six signs, it might have proven fatal. So, the last Burma Shave sign went up: "All these years . . . we've done our part . . . to make your face . . . a work . . . of art . . . Burma Shave."

Now, nearly thirty years since those signs have disappeared, I still recall many of those words of "wits-dom." And this is ironic in a sense because I hold four university degrees and am considered a very educated man; yet I remember Burma Shave jingles better than I do many of the major philosophical statements I've read by Socrates, Plato, Aristotle, Descartes, Kant, and other great thinkers. The explanation of this can probably be found in Thoreau's famous line in *Walden*, "Simplify, simplify, simplify!"

I'm convinced that simplicity was the secret of Jesus' evangelistic success. If you think about it, His entire message was summarized in two words: "Follow me" (Matthew 4:19).

Christ gave us simple words of wisdom that were meant to encourage, as well as to guide us. Consider some of these sayings that you already are familiar with:

"Do not judge, or you too will be judged" (Matthew 7:1).

"No one can serve two masters" (Matthew 6:24).

"Have faith in God" (Mark 11:22).

"No good tree bears bad fruit. . . . The good man brings good things out of the good stored up in his heart" (Luke 6:43-45).

"The man who loves his life will lose it while the man who hates life in this world will keep it for eternal life" (John 12:25).

## SIMPLICITY

Though expressed in simple ways, the messages of Jesus were profound and deep, wise and stimulating. A simple statement, such as a wise man builds his house upon a rock (see Luke 6:48), carries many lessons about life. Readers know that a house built on sand will wash away during a big storm. Similarly, a "house" (be it a family, a career, or a spiritual relationship with God) will also "wash away" if there is no bedrock for a foundation. The lesson here is easy to understand, it is memorable, it is accurate. It succeeds, not in spite of its simplicity but because of it.

I believe we can learn two lessons from the way Christ taught. First, if we want to be wise, we should spend time reading the Scriptures. God has given us the Bible. It is filled with the Old Testament revelations about the coming Messiah and the New Testament sermons, stories, and lessons taught by that Messiah in simple, easy-to-follow ways. Jesus used parables, anecdotes, examples, and familiar expressions to teach us the weighty and profound ways of God. What had seemed complicated and abstruse, Jesus made understandable and clear.

A second lesson is that we should use a similar approach in witnessing when we share the gospel with others. Just as a newborn baby can handle only a diet of milk, so, too, prospective Christians must be "nursed" along in easy ways (see 1 Peter 2:2). It is far better to talk about how one is saved than to become involved in a deep theological debate over the causes of original sin or the discernments related to prophecy. Those meat-and-potatoes subjects can be digested later, at maturity.

As representatives of Christ, we can put His words of wisdom before people the same way the post hole diggers did the Burma Shave signs of old. The signs of life that Jesus gave, however, won't be limited in time the way the Burma Shave signs were. His words are valid for eternity.

Solomon, the wisest man who ever lived, praised the use of simple language that could benefit all: "All the words of my mouth are just. . . . To the discerning all of them are right; they are faultless to those who have knowledge" (Proverbs 8:8, 9).

That's our challenge. We need to read the simple truth Christ gave us, then share it in equally simple ways with others.

"Study your Bible . . . all your days . . . then share it . . . with others . . . in simple ways . . . Burma Shave."

## Chapter Ten

# Discipline

Not long ago I returned to Indiana after having been the keynote speaker at a large business conference in Florida. It had been one of those bookings at which everything had gone right. The audience had loved me. They'd laughed at my jokes, nodded their agreement as I'd hit home on my main points, jotted notes as I had presented my key information, and then had given me a five-minute standing ovation at the end. It had been an incredible experience.

On the plane ride home I began to replay my speech in my mind. Yes, I'd been sharp all right. In fact, I soon began to think that there were probably very few people in the entire country who could have given so grand a speech.

I was feeling pretty self-important by the time I arrived home around midnight. I unlocked the back door and entered through the kitchen. There on the table was a note from my wife:

Sweetheart,

I got too tired to wait up for you. Sorry. You can tell me tomorrow about your trip. I'm sure you did well. Love, Rose.

P.S. Don't forget to take out the garbage.

Those seven little words in that hastily scribbled postscript immediately pulled me back into reality. Within two minutes of having arrived home, I had been reduced from professional orator to household janitor. Ahh, fame—how fleeting.

I did go ahead and take out the garbage that night. And I still am taking out the garbage. Each weekend. Even without a reminder note. Some things in life we have to discipline ourselves to do, like them or not.

I think, however, that all those nights of having to take out the garbage are what made that one night of getting a standing ovation so special. If it had happened all the time, I probably would have complained about that too. ("Oh, do I *have* to fly all the way to Florida again? Please, not another one of those standing-ovation routines. Anything but that! Can't I just *once* stay at home, take out the garbage, and simply be a regular person!")

Our lives as Christians are a lot like that too. In

order to appreciate the special achievements we gain through a life in Christ, we first have to endure a lot of disciplines—mental, spiritual, emotional, and physical. These disciplines can be challenging, rigid, and, at times, even annoying; they demand that we examine ourselves regularly and, when need be, that we "take out the garbage."

Jesus was frequently active in tossing out garbage. When He cleared the temple of the moneychangers, He was tossing out spiritual decay. When He challenged and debated the scribes and elders, He was purging their minds of incorrect mental debris. He came to cleanse the souls of people and to wash them "as white as snow" (Isaiah 1:18).

The Bible tells us that our bodies are the temples of the Lord. If you reside in a mansion, you surely would not scatter trash and rubbish in the hallways, stairwells, and living areas. So, too, our bodies must be clean and clear of life's garbage. Even a small amount of worldly debris will be a detraction from our spiritual beauty.

After my wife and I had been married eighteen years and had worked hard and saved our money, we were able to buy a beautiful house. We looked forward to the day when we would move in. On moving day, the movers accidentally caught a little rock beneath our piano as it was being rolled across the foyer to the living room. The rock tore a long narrow gash into the vinyl flooring.

For the next several weeks many of our friends and relatives came to see our new home. Everyone complimented us on the beautiful woodwork, the spacious rooms, the colorful decorating. And everyone also noticed and asked about the tear in our vinyl floor. Although 99 percent of our house was new and beautiful, that did not keep the one unsightly part from showing. We finally reported the accident to our insurance company and had the vinyl replaced. Only then was the house fully beautiful.

As faithful Christians, we cannot be disciplined in some areas and lax in others. The former does not hide the latter. For example, we may have our tongues under control so that whatever we say is gracious and encouraging to others, but what good is that if we are not fair and honest in our work? Similarly, we may be faithful in our church attendance and in tithing, but what good will that be if we do not work, talk, and live our convictions once we walk outside the church door? The Christian life calls for us to discipline ourselves in all matters and to keep our temples clean.

The apostle Paul taught us how to construct the right kind of temples and how to keep them spotless and free of the world's garbage. Paul's advice was simple: build your temple on the foundation of Jesus Christ and then maintain it as if, indeed, it were Christ's personal home. Each one should be careful how he builds. "For no one can lay any foundation other than the one already laid, which is Jesus Christ. . . . Don't you know that you yourselves are God's temple and that God's Spirit lives in you? . . . God's temple is sacred, and you are that temple" (1 Corinthians 3:10-17).

I need to ask myself each day how I am keeping

house for the Lord. I need to check the nooks and crannies of my personal temple to make sure they are clean. If they are not, I usually find a note left by the Lord. It says, "P.S. Don't forget to take out the garbage."

## Chapter Eleven

# Vision

The Bible warns us that "where there is no vision, the people perish" (Proverbs 29:18, KJV). Many an individual has nearly perished because of shortsightedness. One of the greatest examples was the apostle Paul, whom the Lord gave a graphic object lesson on the value of proper sight-setting.

On the road to Damascus, Paul was given a "heavenly vision" of Jesus. Prior to this, Paul had been persecuting Christians in the name of religion rather than seeking the true will of God. His intent was right, but his focus was not; his zeal was commendable, but his procedures were not. He was spiritually blind to God's purpose and will. As Paul later described the experience, he said that Jesus addressed him from heaven:

" 'I am Jesus, whom you are persecuting,' the Lord replied. 'Now get up and stand on your feet. I have appeared to you to appoint you as a servant and as a witness of what you have seen of me and what I will show you. I will rescue you from your own people and from the Gentiles. I am sending you to open their eyes and turn them from darkness to light' " (Acts 26:15-18).

During His earthly ministry, Jesus frequently gave sight to the blind. Conversely, after confronting Paul, He caused Paul to *become* blind. This seeming paradox was actually logical. For several days Paul was forced to stumble around in total darkness, a helpless man, lacking direction and vision. No doubt he feared being left alone, feared being injured, feared not being able to care for himself.

Jesus had a purpose in this. He used Paul's physical blindness to illustrate the spiritual condition of the Gentiles. Stumbling in spiritual darkness, they were as blind to the truth as he had been. They needed a guide, someone to give them a heavenly vision.

And so it was that Paul's eyes were opened twice. He first was given a new vision of God's will for his life, and then his physical vision was restored so that he could do God's will. Paul not only shared this new vision with others, he maintained it for himself the rest of his life. Near the end of his life, Paul could say that he had set his sight on the prize of heaven, and he had run the good race in order to attain that prize (see 2 Timothy 4:7). Jesus had taught him to maintain a righteous vision. That, in turn, would promote a righteous life.

Jesus Himself had led a life that was guided by a "heavenly vision." He came with a goal of fulfilling the laws of Moses and the predictions of the prophets regarding Himself (see Luke 24:44) and then of returning to the right hand of the Father.

Having a vision of where you are going and how you are going to get there not only prepares you for a long life, but for a short one as well. We all expect to live long lives and then to have eternal life with Christ in heaven. If, however, our vision is set on that heavenly home all along, then, even if our lives are cut short, it will make no difference. The same vision will direct us to the same destination.

I had this brought to my attention in a startling way. I was at Camp Lake, Wisconsin, giving a series of lectures on writing techniques to a wonderful group of missionaries, pastors, and other people in full-time Christian service. One of my students was a spry, diminutive, gray-haired woman from Kansas. Her name was Margaret, and I got to know her well. When she found out I was from Fort Wayne, Indiana, she bonded to me immediately.

"I'm a Hoosier myself," she explained with a proud tilt of the head and a quick wink. "I've lived in many states, but I've always carried Indiana in my heart. It's home. I'll be going back again soon."

"Oh, really?" I said. "A visit?"

"Retirement," she corrected me. "My hubby and I will be settling in Wabash, not far from where you are in Fort Wayne. I'm really looking forward to it. I've got big plans. Indeed, big plans."

"Such as writing your life story?" I asked.

She grinned, slightly self-conscious. "You heard me say that when we did the introductions, didn't you? I've always loved writing, but I haven't had much time for it. I've kept journals and diaries, though. I won't lack for material once I get started. Oh, the stories I have to tell."

I pumped her to share these stories as we sat together at meals or walked to classes together. Truly, she had had a fascinating life and career. She'd been a wife, mom, and grandmother. She'd worked with the poor, the uneducated, the homeless. She'd taught at a Christian school, helped develop mission work, and had been a song leader and prayer partner. She'd done it all.

After a mere two days I began to feel as though I'd known this woman all my life. I invited her to visit me once she moved back to Indiana. I promised to read sections of her manuscript and to help guide her writings. This seemed to please her immensely. She promised to "look me up" later that year once her retirement had started.

That same evening an ice-cream social was planned for the participants in the writers' group. I wrote my address and phone number on a piece of paper to give to Margaret when I saw her at the fellowship time.

I got there early and waited, watching for Margaret. When she didn't show up with some of the lady friends she was sharing a room with, I asked about her.

"Margaret has asthma, and it's acting up a bit," I was told. "She's in the lady's room downstairs splashing cold water on her face. She'll be here soon."

I waited another twenty minutes, but still Margaret did not arrive. Then, suddenly, flashing red lights and the wail of an ambulance siren interrupted the social. Everyone rushed to the window.

Before long the director of the conference center entered the room, his face pale. With a strained voice he made an announcement.

"Margaret, our friend and dear sister in Christ, is dead. We'll need everyone to stay inside while the body is transferred to the ambulance."

I was numb. *Unbelievable! Not Margaret. Margaret? No, surely not. That's impossible.*

I somehow found my way to a chair. Margaret? Dead? My new friend was dead? I had talked to her that morning, and she had been so full of life. Now she was dead. How could this be possible?

"It's quite a shock, isn't it?" someone said softly.

I looked up. It was one of Margaret's roommates. She sat down next to me.

"She liked you, you know," she whispered. "She said you were a delightful young man."

I couldn't help myself. I smiled at that. I was forty-one years old, but Margaret had thought of me as "a young man." Even in death she was a charmer.

"The timing seems so wrong," I mumbled, mostly to myself. "She was almost ready to retire. She was going to move back to Indiana, near her grandchildren. She planned to start writing a book—her life story. She . . . she had so much to live for. Know what I mean?"

The older woman smiled. "I think I do. But she also had so much to die for."

This seemed paradoxical. "How's that? I don't think I'm following you."

"Are you familiar with Philippians 1:21?"

I nodded. "For to me, to live is Christ and to die is gain," I quoted from memory. "The words of the apostle Paul."

"Yes," said the woman. "But they could just as easily have been spoken by Margaret. Every day of her life was dedicated to serving the Lord. She did it in the way she interacted with other people. Her whole life was spent that way. And, had she continued to live another twenty years, it would have continued to be spent that way."

"But she isn't going to be here another twenty years," I said flatly.

"And that's *her* gain," my companion injected quickly. She reminded me that because Margaret had set her vision on her heavenly home all along, she had a crown and a mansion waiting for her in heaven. In heaven, she would have reunions with old friends and the chance to stand face to face with the One she had served so long.

"Look at it this way, Dennis," she continued. "Now your heavenly reward will be a little better than before. As a Christian, you already had the reward of a mansion and a crown to look forward to—especially the reward of seeing Jesus. Now you will be able to look forward to seeing Margaret again."

The woman was right. Because Margaret had had a vision of where she was headed, my own vision had been enhanced. Even the friend's final words emphasized this. She said I could "look forward" to "seeing" Margaret again. How true.

Christ spoke a great deal about vision. He warned us not to do good things just to be noticed (see Matthew 6:1). He told us not to look at the small problems of our neighbors but to the big problems within ourselves (see Matthew 7:3).

Jesus had a singular vision: to obey the Scriptures and to be prepared to return to the right hand of the Father. In using the Jesus Effect as it applies to vision, we, too, should *see* the Scriptures as a lamp unto our feet and a light unto our path, and we should focus on heaven as our destination point. With these two traveling aids, our arrival is guaranteed.

# Chapter Twelve

# Admonition

In many places the Bible teaches that Christians have an obligation to "admonish one another" (Romans 15:14, KJV). The word *admonish* has a dual meaning: sometimes it means "to reprove or challenge an individual about his or her views or behavior"; other times it means "to endorse or encourage someone."

Bible translators use the word *admonition* in both of these meanings, depending on the context. If a fellow Christian needs to be brought back into line after having strayed from the disciplines of the faith, that person is to be admonished about his error; but the admonition must be as loving as it is honest and direct (see 2 Thessalonians 3:15). If a person is to be admonished to keep up an already established righteous work, this is to be done with the endorsement of Scripture and the sweetness of song (see Colossians 3:16).

Since admonition is a part of the Christian duty, it behooves us to consider biblical examples of how, when, and from whom it should be given.

Years ago my sister had a poster in her room that read, "Learn to make a decision—to lead, to follow, or to get out of the way!" In adhering to that adage, she eventually became a college dean at the relatively young age of thirty-two.

Sometimes I wish that such posters hung in a lot of offices, family rooms, and churches. In one terse admonition, that poster summarizes the key to all work success: namely, if you are a leader, then lead with strength and confidence; if you are a follower, then provide reliable, high-quality support; and if you want no part in the project, have the common courtesy to keep your opinions to yourself and to stand out of the way of other people's progress.

The habit of not criticizing a project in which you're not directly involved, is harder to develop than you might think. I struggle with it constantly. I catch myself saying to one of my children, "No, no, don't do it that way. Here, watch me. I'll show you the proper way." Or I'll say to a co-worker, "You're spending too much time on the wrong activity. You need to focus your priority on this project over here."

It's so easy to criticize. We do it constantly. But we need to break that habit. In Psalm 19:14 the psalmist prays, "May the words of my mouth and the meditation of my heart be pleasing in your sight, O Lord." Critical words can be devastating, so we must be cautious.

Recently, I was approached by the woman who had been my daughter's first-grade teacher many years ago. She said, "Several years back, you did something that really helped me become a better teacher."

"Oh, really?" I asked. "What was that?"

"I had sent a note home with my students," she explained, "and I really hadn't taken the time to proofread it. You returned the note to me and pointed out that I had made a spelling error and a grammar error. You told me I was a terrific teacher and that your daughter was greatly benefiting from being in my class. You then said you didn't want *anything* to have a negative influence on my career, so you quickly wanted to show me that hasty note writing was not in my best interest. I was so moved by your sincere concern for my career and your tactful way of pointing out my errors, I made it a habit to take more time with my writing from that point on."

I was amazed that something I had done so long ago could still be having such a positive effect on this woman's life. It made me realize, however, that harsh, critical words could have caused negative effects just as long lasting. James 3:2 came to mind: "If anyone is never at fault in what he says, he is a perfect man."

A story in the book of Nehemiah illustrates how negative criticism can demoralize people, hurt their feelings, and decrease their productivity.

Nehemiah had returned to Jerusalem because he was grieved that the city lay in ruins and, thus, was defenseless against marauders. Nehemiah rallied the local citizens and convinced them that by working together, they could clear away the debris and then restore the beauty of their city. Their first project would be to rebuild the mighty wall that had protected Jerusalem.

The people became enthusiastic about the project. They hauled away rubble and brought in new stone. They carved wooden beams for gates and cast bolts and bars in metal. As their progress became evident, several enemies of the Jews became worried over this success and laid plans to impede the rebuilding project.

The leaders of the Samaritans and the Ammonites began by ridiculing the Jews and their project. The wall supposedly was so poorly constructed that a fox could undo the repair. Before long, the Jews began to believe this negative propaganda and became discouraged.

In desperation, Nehemiah prayed to God for wisdom and encouragement. He then encouraged the people by reminding them that the Lord, "Who is great and awesome," was on their side (Nehemiah 4:14). The people returned to work, even though they had to hold a weapon in one hand and work with the other, in order to thwart the threatened attack. They continued working as both guards and builders until the wall was rebuilt and the doors were set in the gates.

How about you? Have you ever halted the progress on someone's wall by something critical you have said? It's better to lead or support a project—but if you can't do that, guard carefully what you say about it. You never know when the wall you have criticized was being built under God's command.

Jesus was not afraid to rebuke and admonish when such was needed; however, His first priority was to uplift and restore. When asked to pass judgment on the woman caught in adultery, He responded that, in different ways, the woman's accusers were equally guilty. He then graciously told the woman to cease her sinful ways and to start a new life—uncondemned.

As we analyze the way Jesus gave admonition, we can find three guidelines:

1. *His admonitions were always for other people's well-being.* For example, when Peter cut off Malchus's ear during Jesus' arrest, Jesus healed the ear. He then warned Peter that to live by the sword was to die by the sword (see Matthew 26:52).

Similarly, when Martha complained to Jesus that her sister Mary was not helping with the meal preparation, Jesus gently corrected Martha by reminding her that household duties were less important than listening to Jesus' words. It was better for Martha to join Mary at the feet of Jesus and to benefit from His teachings (see Luke 10:38-42).

Indeed, Jesus did admonish people, but it was always for their own well-being.

2. *His admonitions were always timely.* Jesus never carried a grudge or licked old wounds. If a

problem arose, He would address it immediately and put an end to the matter. When Philip asked Jesus to show them the Father, Jesus did not stomp away angrily and brood for several days about Philip's unbelief. Instead, He answered immediately, "Anyone who has seen me has seen the Father," and gently admonished Philip for his lack of faith and insight.

In my own life I have discovered the time to deal with a matter needing correction is when the problem arises. In 1982 I bought a home in Fort Wayne that had been unoccupied for ten months. The neighborhood youngsters had gotten into the habit of cutting through my backyard to get to my neighbor's house. Often I would yell from my windows for the kids not to cut across my property any longer, but when my back was turned, they would run through again. This made me angrier and angrier.

Finally, one day I could stand it no more. I drove around the block to the family whose property bordered my backyard. In a raised voice I complained to the owners about how their children and their children's friends were continually trespassing on my property and trampling my new grass. To my great surprise, these parents apologized for the intrusion, promised to forbid their children from taking shortcuts through my backyard, and even offered to pay me if my lawn had been damaged. They were very friendly and totally cooperative. How foolish I had been to allow this problem to frustrate me for months when I could have immediately taken my complaint to my neighbor and had it solved. Like Jesus, I now try to give admonitions at the moment a problem arises.

3. *His admonitions were reinforced by His own actions.* Whatever words of correction or caution or chastisement Jesus gave to others, He was always willing to accept as rules for Himself too. When He admonished His followers that "they should always pray" (Luke 18:1), He heeded His own admonition and spent days in the wilderness fasting and praying, as well as long nights on His knees in prayer. When He reminded others to "honor your father and mother" (Luke 18:20), He practiced this principle in His own life by working as a carpenter with Joseph, by fulfilling the mission given to Him by God the Father, and by caring for Mary, even to the point of delegating the apostle John to tend to her needs after the crucifixion. He admonished no one in any matter that He, Himself, was not ready to be obedient to as well.

When my son Nathan was only four, he would often keep his eyes open and look around church whenever our pastor would be leading in prayer. I reminded Nathan several times that he should close his eyes, bow his head, and show reverence toward God during prayer time. Being a child, he sometimes forgot my admonitions. One day when he was looking around during prayer, I placed my hand on the back of his head and gently bowed his head. That worked very effectively in making Nathan understand that prayer time was concentration time.

A few weeks after that, I was late to the service because I had helped an elderly gentleman walk up the stairs to the church. When I finally joined my family, the pastor was already leading in prayer for the morning offering. As he prayed, I hastily reached for my wallet, took out my offering, put it into the offering envelope, and then began to write my name on the envelope. Nathan looked up at me just as I was writing my name during prayer. He quickly reached over, placed his hand on the back of my head, and pushed my face down into a praying position.

For the life of me, I couldn't help but chuckle. The little guy was right. If I had insisted that he bow his head reverently during prayer time, I should have been ready to follow my own admonition. I learned a good lesson that day about the need to "walk what you talk."

Solomon wrote, "There is a time for everything, and a season for every activity under heaven." "A time to be silent, and a time to speak" (Ecclesiastes 3:1, 7). Jesus was a living example of this principle. He was tolerant in His silence, but when admonition was needed and beneficial, He did not hesitate to speak. And having spoken, He adhered to His own advice. He set a good example for us to follow.

Chapter

# Thirteen

# Success

Recently, after I gave a one-hour motivation speech at a gathering of church workers, I was approached by a woman who stated coldly, "You need to learn that God is not keeping score regarding our accomplishments here on earth. My heart is pure and my eyes are on Christ. That's what really matters, sir!"

I smiled, nodded my agreement, and said, "Indeed—for *your* life. But what about your next-door neighbor and your dentist and your letter carrier and your beautician and your grocer? Are *their* hearts pure; are *their* eyes on Christ? If not, I guarantee you that your salvation is not going to save them. It is your witnessing that is going to make a difference. Don't equate confidence about your own spiritual situation with behavior that is glorifying to God. If you've found salvation for yourself, you are only halfway successful; now you must help others find it. Do some work!"

Noted management specialist Philip B. Crosby once stated, "Not failing is not the same as succeeding." At first reading, that statement may seem paradoxical. Upon deeper reflection, however, you will discover that it states a great truth. Phrased another way it might be said, "There is no status quo. You are either moving ahead, or you are losing ground."

The same thing is true of the Christian life. There is no such thing as success in general; there is only success at *something*. Whatever your particular talent, it should be directed toward ministry or service. If you are *not* advancing toward the goal—or, far worse, if you are drifting away from it—you are failing.

Now note, I did not say your goal had to be something that turns the world upside down. All I said was that you should *have* a goal and you should be moving toward achieving it. God will bless even the smallest efforts, if they are made sincerely. The widow of Zarephath used her last meal and oil to feed the prophet Elijah (see 1 Kings 17:7-16). Another widow donated two mites to the temple treasury (see Mark 12:41-44; Luke 21:1-4). Both gifts were considered priceless in God's eyes, even though by human standards they seemed insignificant.

God does not want the service of a "blow hard." I once knew a man who boasted that after he received his holiday bonus, he was going to buy all new choir robes for the church. He also promised that once he was transferred to working second shift, he would help the pastor make calls on the needy. He talked of great things, but he never got around to doing any of them. Meanwhile, an elderly woman in our church worked faithfully as a nursery helper every Wednesday and weekend service. Her faithful work as an assistant was of far greater value than the unachieved big plans of the talkative man.

Ecclesiastes 5:3, 4 explains, "As a dream [goal] comes when there are many cares [work], so the speech of a fool when there are many words. When you make a vow to God, do not delay in fulfilling it. He has no pleasure in fools."

God is pleased by successful workers. When David raised up a great army (his work) and went out to reclaim the land of Israel, God gave him victory. When Solomon built the great temple (his work), God blessed it. When Joshua attacked the inhabitants of Canaan (his work), God gave him the land. When Nehemiah developed a plan to rebuild the wall of Jerusalem (his work), God protected the workers.

Conversely, God "has no pleasure in fools" who neglect to do the work He has called them to do and equipped them to succeed at. When Moses was too meek to speak before Pharaoh, God took the gift of oratory from Moses and gave it to Aaron. When Jonah ran from the assignment to preach in Nineveh, God created a great fish to swallow him.

When John Mark could not maintain the pace of aggressive evangelism that Paul had set, Paul dismissed him from the work—and received no rebuke from God for doing so.

God's people and His churches do not honor Him when they are complacent and neutral. God gave a message to the church at Laodicea that needs to be heeded by all churches and all Christians: "I know your deeds, that you are neither cold nor hot. I wish you were either one or the other! So, because you are lukewarm—and neither hot nor cold—I am about to spit you out of my mouth" (Revelation 3:15, 16). This sounds amazingly similar to Crosby's admonition that not failing is not the same as succeeding. God's will is for us *to succeed* at a God-honoring work.

Jesus succeeded in all He set out to accomplish here on earth. Not only that, but He spent time teaching His followers that they, too, should succeed at some work for God the Father.

Jesus explained it once with a little parable recorded in Luke 13:6-9. A man owned a lovely vineyard with a fig tree planted among the vines. The fig tree had many branches and many lush green leaves and many deep, strong roots, yet it produced no fruit. The landowner had been patient with the tree for three growing seasons, but in none of those years did the tree yield figs.

Finally, the landowner told his head gardener to chop down the tree, dig out the roots, and plant a new tree on the spot so that eventually fruit would be produced in that section of the orchard. Understanding his employer's frustration, the head gardener suggested an alternative plan. He asked that he be allowed to irrigate and fertilize the tree one more year. If the tree did not bear fruit the following year, then indeed it should be chopped down.

We should take this parable as a warning. If we are an unproductive tree planted in one of God's vineyards (a church, a Christian youth group, an evangelistic outreach), we are actually taking up room where someone more productive could be serving and ministering. God, the patient gardener, wants to give us yet another chance. He wants to encourage us to sink our roots into His Word and then become productive for His ministry. However, if we will not heed His suggestions and encouragements, then He will agree that it may be best for us to be removed from our vineyard of ministry.

How about you? Are you succeeding at anything? Sooner or later harvest time will come. When it does, what will you show—abundance or barrenness? It has to be one or the other, because not failing is not the same as succeeding.

So it is, then, that the Jesus Effect applies to success this way: first, we must be like Jesus in completing our mission and work on this earth as He did; and second, we must share this message with others as He did and let them know that there is no place for complacency in the work of the Lord.

Chapter

# Fourteen

# Composure

Seventeen years after I came home from military service in Vietnam, I was in Washington, D.C., on business. I phoned some friends who lived in the area, and they invited me to their home for dinner. After a pleasant evening together, they offered to drive me back to my hotel and to show me some of the tourist attractions along the way.

I had never been in the capital before, so I was awestruck by the sight of the Jefferson and Lincoln memorials illuminated for night viewing. I was equally impressed by the White House, the Washington Monument, and the Library of Congress. I don't believe any American can look at such grand structures and not feel a special pride and patriotism.

I wasn't prepared, however, for my first visit to "The Wall"—the Vietnam War Memorial. When my friends told me we were going to park the car and walk up to the wall, I felt hesitant, as if this experience threatened to be negative. I hadn't thought about the war in a long time; I wondered whether seeing the names of friends on that wall might unnerve me. Usually, I can maintain my composure under any circumstances. But walking toward that wall flooded me with memories of why I had volunteered to serve in Vietnam and how it had changed my life.

## One soldier's memories

I have seen my father cry only twice. One time was at his mother's funeral. The other was on the day I left for Vietnam.

Dad had accepted both situations with resolute understanding. This was the way life was: old people died; good men fought against evil. Neither was a preferable circumstance, but both were necessary if the world was to continue with balance. You could cry about it, but you couldn't run from it.

He hadn't. At his mother's funeral, despite the wrenching personal agony he felt, he personally saw to it that every detail was attended to with dignity, loving tribute, and in a manner my grandmother would have found tasteful. Dad was fifty-one at the time.

When he was seventeen he had stepped forward

to join the navy, to fight against the enemy. It was 1944. He was told that he was too young, that he would need his father's signature on a release form. His father had cried that day, but he had signed the form. There was no avoiding it. This was the way of good men. They always came forward when needed to fight against evil. Fathers had no right to restrain them. His hadn't.

Twenty-six years later, mine hadn't either.

It was January 2, 1971. I was a PFC (private first class) at home on leave after seven months of duty at Fort Knox, Kentucky. The family Christmas back in Michigan had been wonderful. But that day was my mother's birthday, and I was catching a plane to California en route to my new duty station in Long Binh, South Vietnam.

As I rechecked my orders, I wasn't even sure I was pronouncing the name of my new duty station correctly. I had studied Spanish, not Vietnamese, in college. Perhaps now that seemed like a poor choice. But at least it had been my choice. Like joining the army. I hadn't been drafted. That hadn't been necessary. Good men always came forward to fight against evil. It was the way.

As a PFC my military job code was 71M20, chaplain's assistant. The position had come to me almost by process of elimination: I could type; I had a college degree; I was a trained musician; and I was *not* a conscientious objector. These factors made me *eligible* for a 71M20 slot. What probably clinched it, however, was my psychological profile interview. I don't think the poor psychologist knew where else to assign me.

"These are general questions that we ask all new soldiers," he explained to me. "It's my job to find out something about you—your personality—and then to suggest some job assignments with which you would be compatible."

I nodded.

"Tell me, Private Hensley, how much social drinking do you do?"

"Abstainer since birth," I replied.

He stared at me a moment, as though he had never before heard the expression. He pondered it, but then wrote down *teetotaler*.

"Do you smoke?"

"No."

"Use profanity?"

"No."

"Like to gamble?"

"No."

He paused a moment, scratched his cheek, and glanced down a list of military job categories. It was obvious I wasn't going to be material for motor pool or drill sergeant schools.

"Have you ever considered Officer Candidate School?"

"Forget it," I said. Then, remembering I was no longer a civilian, I rephrased my reply. "I mean, no, thank you, sir."

"Are you bitter about being in the army?"

"I can't tell," I said honestly.

He wrinkled his forehead questioningly.

"I've been in only four days."

That made him frown.

"It's been fine so far, though," I added, trying to appease him.

"Tell me this," he said, putting his pen aside and leaning back in his chair. "How do you feel about war, about people killing people?"

"Which question do you want me to answer first?" I asked. "How I feel about war, or how I feel about people killing people?"

"You don't equate the two?"

"Do you?"

"*I'll* ask the questions, please."

Again, I nodded. "Right."

I took a moment to collect my thoughts.

"I'm a linguist by training," I said at last. "I study and analyze words. It's my job to plumb the depth of the word's meaning before I use it. When you ask how I feel about people killing people, I have to ask for clarification. I have completely different views and opinions on such things as murder, assassination, and execution. Which do you want to hear first?"

The psychologist reached over and turned off a tape recorder.

"Look," he said, "these interviews are supposed to last only fifteen minutes. Just tell me if you have any qualms about fighting the Communists in South Vietnam."

"No," I said. "That's why I enlisted."

Why is it that the obvious always seems so hard to see, I wondered?

"All right then," he said, rubbing his hands together, "I'm going to suggest that you agree to serve in the Chaplaincy Corps as a chaplain's assistant.

By the way, how good are you with a rifle?"

"Sir?" I said, somewhat confused by the contrast of the question.

"Are you a good shot or not?" he repeated.

I shrugged my shoulders. "I grew up in a suburb," I said almost apologetically. "I've never fired a rifle, except for a .22 at Boy Scout camp once."

The doctor weighed that mentally.

"Then take a word of advice, soldier," he said. "Pay close attention to what those drill sergeants teach you during the next six weeks. Very, *very* close attention."

At the end of basic training I was given orders to remain at Fort Knox for OJT (on-the-job training) at Triangle Chapel. I reported to Chaplain (Major) Merrill O. Challman on August 1, 1970. He waved off my salute, motioned for me to stand at ease, and then looked me over.

"How good are you with a rifle?" he asked, first thing.

*Déjà vu*, I thought. *Here we go again.*

I said, "Marksman, sir."

"Not expert?" he pressed.

"No, sir. But I missed by only two points."

He smiled at that. "Well, that's impressive. You've had a lot of experience with guns then."

I shook my head. "No, sir, not until six weeks ago. But that worked to my advantage. I had no bad habits to break. I just did exactly what the drill sergeants said to do. I learned by the book. And the book was right."

"Good," he said. "All right, here's a rundown of your duties around here."

I scanned the list of chores such as cleaning the altar silver, waxing the floor, answering the phone, typing correspondence, and setting up counseling appointments.

"And I want you to spend two hours each week on the target range," he said. "After you finally qualify as an Expert on the M-16 rifle, I want you to move on to the M-79 grenade launcher and then the M-60 machine gun."

I felt puzzled. These seemed odd requests from "a man of the cloth." I ventured, "In all due respect, sir, why do I need to become a weapons expert just to be the chapel's janitor and your receptionist?"

He put his hand on my shoulder in an almost sympathetic way. "You'll know soon enough," he said. "Trust me. It's important."

It *was* important. In fact, it was a matter of life and death, or shall I say lives and deaths—my own and the chaplain's.

Like medics, chaplains were "excused from" having to (read that "forbidden to") bear arms even in combat situations. However, they did have one other source of protection besides prayer—the chaplain's assistant. Wherever a chaplain went throughout the war zone, his assistant went with him, usually with an M-16 rifle in hand and ammunition bandoleers crisscrossed over his chest.

In other words, the same fellow who had been a receptionist and janitor while serving stateside quickly became a bodyguard when he arrived in Vietnam. If he was a *good* bodyguard, the chaplain he was assigned to would make it through the war. If he was an *extremely good* bodyguard, the assistant would make it through the war too. And that was why Chaplain Challman saw to it that I became an extremely good bodyguard.

While at Fort Knox with Chaplain Challman, I was part of the Armor Corps. When my orders for Vietnam came through, I was reassigned to the military police.

Chaplain Challman gave me some simple advice on the day we parted company. "Pray for the protection of God," he said, "but never forget the wickedness of man."

My father said something similar to that when he hugged me on that last day. His eyes were red, and a tear was rolling down one cheek. "Keep your Bible *and* your rifle in ready reach at all times," he cautioned.

I promised I would. And then he let me go.

The flights to Vietnam were long. I had a chance to slowly, carefully replay the memory tapes of my life in an effort to discover how it was that, at age twenty-one, of my own choosing, I was en route to a country I had never visited, yet planned to defend against an invader with my life.

From Michigan to California I pondered the problem. From California to Hawaii I eliminated the obvious answers and simplistic explanation. Much later, somewhere over the Pacific Ocean between Hawaii and Vietnam, I found my solutions. I ultimately decided that it all came down to my fourth-grade Sunday School teacher, Joe Jenkins, Jr., and a 1966 trip I made to what was then East Germany. An odd combination of factors perhaps, but then what in life isn't?

When I was nine, I'd had perfect attendance for a year in Sunday school. My teacher, Mr. Jenkins, had given me a New Testament as a reward. He had admonished me to put it in my hip pocket and carry it with me every day, wherever I went. One never knew, he told me, where God would direct, and it could very well be that there would be many chances to witness to people if I would just keep that New Testament handy.

I was young, and I took his words literally. I began to carry that New Testament in all my clothing—in my school trousers, in my summer baseball uniform and, of course, in my dress slacks. Years passed and I maintained the practice, more out of habit than conscious effort. We moved from Detroit to Bay City, and the New Testament also moved (on my person). It was always with me.

Just as Mr. Jenkins had predicted, chances to witness did arise: sometimes at school, sometimes at summer camp, sometimes at college. I even led my future wife to the Lord in 1969, thanks to that handy little dog-eared New Testament.

Without consciously knowing it, I had become a missionary while in the fourth grade. A dozen years later, that same small black-covered New Testament was still in my hip pocket as I flew, now dressed in an army uniform, toward Vietnam. From now on I would be witnessing not only to my own people but also to others of new races and nationalities. I felt prepared, even *called*, if you will.

But there was more to my motivation. I also came to realize that I was an anti-Communist. And I was as much an anti-Communist in my own way as my father had been an anti-Nazi during his war. Only now I knew why. And I suddenly understood a lot more about my father.

You see, in 1966, after graduating from high school, I had spent the summer touring Europe on my own. While there, I had taken a ten-day trip through East Germany. I saw loading areas where Jews had been put on trains to be taken to concentration camps.

It upset me. That never should have been tolerated, I thought. Where had the good men been then? Why hadn't more come forward? Where had the Davids been, unafraid of the giants; the Moseses, unafraid of the oppressors; the Peters, ready to pull a sword from the hip at any sign of wrongdoing? My father had been a good man—a good Christian man. He, obviously, had said, "This must stop. Now! It's barbaric. I *am* my brother's keeper. This cannot be condoned." And then he had stepped forward. I was proud of that.

It wasn't that good men lusted for war, I realized. They craved peace. But to obtain peace, good men often had to serve as the peace*makers*. Nobody liked the role. But, like Gideon, they accepted it with equal feelings of awe and bafflement, amazed to think they could make a difference.

But I really didn't worry about making a difference in Vietnam. I just accepted my assignment, the same way I had once accepted that little black New Testament. God would provide the opportunities. All I knew was that concentration camps, torture, oppression, and war were now being used by the oppressors in Southeast Asia the same way they had earlier been used by oppressors in Central Europe. And it was time once again for good men to come forward. My composure was intact. I was doing the right thing.

According to the army records I did make a difference during my years in Vietnam. Perhaps. I flew in helicopters and protected chaplains who were going to and from the distant firebase camps. It was rough at times, and they gave me the Bronze Star Medal and two Vietnamese service medals for being an *extremely good* bodyguard. Actually, the motivation came quite naturally at the time. I just wanted to stay alive. But I accepted the medals and wrote home to my father about it. He understood completely. A good man did what he had to do.

And I did eight months' duty working with a chaplain who was assigned to a stockade. I helped to organize prisoner choirs, I wrote letters home for prisoners, and the chaplain and I were just there whenever a prisoner was lonely and needed someone to talk to. It was sorrowful at times. They gave me the Army Commendation Medal, the National Defense Ribbon, and the Good Conduct Medal for that and promoted me to Specialist Fifth Class (sergeant). I accepted it all, but I began to cross off the days on my calendar. It was a long war, and even a man who strives to do good grows weary in time.

During that year in Vietnam, I witnessed to many Americans and many Vietnamese. I also physically resisted the Communist takeover. I did what I could, which most of the time didn't seem adequate.

But after I was sent home in 1972, I sat in front

of my television set and viewed newsreels of the Communist takeover of South Vietnam. I saw innocent people killed in cold blood. I saw farmers driven off their land and cast adrift in leaky ships. I watched these helpless "boat people" drown because they were forbidden to return to their own shores.

And I said, "We were right to have helped those people. *I* was right to have helped those people. But why did we stop? Why did we stop helping?"

And the unspoken answer became obvious: because good men quit coming forward to fight against evil.

All these memories came back to me that night, seventeen years after the war, as I approached the Vietnam War Memorial. And suddenly the old confidence came back to me that what my buddies and I had done had been the right thing. My composure was intact because my heart was at peace.

I located the names of three men I had known well who had been killed in battle. Seeing their names brought a smile of fond memories to my face. The man reading the names on the wall had graying temples and some lines around his eyes. Yet, my buddies were still young in my memory.

"Rest easy, guys," I whispered. "Your lives counted for something. You were good men. And you came forward."

As I recall that event, it makes me see parallel situations in the quiet composure of Christ. He was often criticized by observers, yet He continued to be devoted to what He knew He was called to do. He was frequently questioned as to His motives and goals, yet He always responded calmly and rationally. He was made a public mockery, yet He had the presence of mind to ask His heavenly Father to forgive those who were torturing and berating Him. He began His work on earth knowing the danger and fatigue and ridicule that lay ahead of Him, yet He remained composed and steadfast under all situations because He knew His cause was just and that His actions were noble. And like the men whose names are on the Vietnam War Memorial, His deed influenced others even after His death.

Chapter
# Fifteen

# Mission

After giving an address at a Christian college, I was approached by a young man who was a senior at that school.

"Your message was very motivating," he told me. "After hearing you, I've decided to make my life available to God for service as a foreign missionary. I'm not going to volunteer to become a missionary; *however*, I'm going to leave that door open in case the Lord should specifically call me to do that."

"I've got a better idea," I challenged him. "Why don't you proceed with plans to become a missionary and stop only if God specifically closes that door to you?"

The young man's eyes widened in surprise. He began to stammer. "Well . . . I . . . I always planned to wait on the Lord's leading."

I smiled. "And the Lord is waiting on *your service*. He's called all of us to fish for souls. Whether you use a net, a rod and reel, or a harpoon is up to you. God doesn't care. What He doesn't need, however, is a bystander. Be aggressive, not passive in your service to Him."

The young man walked away from me, his head lowered in thought. I'm sure that my response to his statement did not please him. He was one of numerous Christians I have met who are happy in their service to the Lord—as long as He requires no service. They are glad to serve in the Lord's army, as long as the battle produces no stress.

Many people are like that. After a year of combat duty in South Vietnam, I was discharged from the U.S. Army in early 1972. The war was winding down, and the troops were coming back to America. Many of my buddies tried to talk me into signing up for the reserves. The only commitment was one meeting per month and two weeks of summer training. Each veteran who signed up would draw salary based on his highest earned rank. It sounded like easy money, but I ultimately decided not to sign up.

For the next three years, whenever I would see some of my former service pals, they would tell me about all the extra money they were taking in each month by being a reservist. One fellow had used the money to finance a second car. Another had bought some fancy clothes, and yet another had purchased a color TV and a stereophonic sound system. They chided me for not having joined the reserves when they had.

"But what if a war breaks out?" I asked. "You'll be called up for duty."

They laughed. "War? *What* war? We've already been at war. There's not going to be another war. We have it made. All we have to do is put on the uniform now and then and take home the pay. It's easy."

And so it was. For a time. Then in rapid succession the U.S. became involved in several military conflicts—the North Korean border clash, the Iranian hostage crisis, the invasion of Grenada, the air strike against Libya, and Operation Desert Storm in the Middle East. Time and again my friends were put on alert status or were actually called up for active duty. They groaned and complained each time they had to leave home.

"Why are you complaining?" I asked one of my friends. "You knew there was a possibility this could happen."

With a sigh, he responded, "It's a lot easier to play at being a soldier than actually having to serve as a soldier. Now, it's serious."

That was very true of my soldier friend's situation. But it was equally true of the situation of the college student who had spoken to me about becoming a missionary. For the student, it was easy to play at being a committed Christian as long as all he had to do was stay in America and go to classes with his friends. However, when I challenged him to leave his friends and family behind and go to a faraway land to "fight the good fight" for Christ, it became serious. Too serious, in fact, for him to handle. He had turned his back on me and had walked away.

Now, you may feel that I spoke too bluntly to the young student, but, for a fact, I learned to speak that way by copying Jesus. In Matthew 8:21, 22 we read: "Another man, one of his disciples, said unto him, 'Lord, first let me go and bury my father.' But Jesus told him, 'Follow me, and let the [spiritually] dead bury their own [physically] dead.' "

Nowhere in the Scriptures do we find Jesus saying that accepting a mission in His name will be easy. Instead, He has said that His followers may find themselves homeless (see Matthew 8:20), at odds with family members (see Matthew 10:36), burdened with responsibilities (see Matthew 11:29), tempted by false prophets (see Matthew 24:5), and mocked and persecuted (see Matthew 5:11, 12).

Anyone who sits on the sidelines and professes to be open to God's leading, yet is not willing to take a step toward actively serving Him, is actually nothing more than a spiritual coward. Understand this: there are no reservists in God's army. We are all assigned to front-line duty—and the war is already raging.

To accept a mission (be it youth leader in the local church or evangelist in a distant land) is to enter the battle zone. It requires total commitment. Only those persons willing to sacrifice everything will succeed in carrying out their missions.

In 1961 President John F. Kennedy made a plea for young Americans to join the Peace Corps and to pledge two years of their lives to working in underdeveloped countries. Initially, many thousands of people from ages eighteen to thirty rushed forward to volunteer. Their noble aims were to share their strength and knowledge with less fortunate people. They envisioned two years of exciting adventure in Portugal or Tahiti or Mexico.

Reality was something quite different, however. Volunteers for the Peace Corps had to endure several weeks of boot camp, where they lived under rugged conditions. This was followed by weeks of intensive language training. Finally, they received their assignments: building a cement-block medical clinic in a remote Honduran village or digging irrigation ditches by hand in a desolate Egyptian settlement in the Arabian Desert.

Just as quickly as they had come forward to volunteer, hundreds of young people who had led pampered and indulged lives were just as quick to resign and return home. Those who remained helped to form a noble enterprise that accomplished many worthwhile projects around the world. But many *more* projects could have been completed if those weak-spirited volunteers who had resigned had truly been committed to completing the mission they had accepted.

Jesus had to deal with similar situations. A rich young ruler bowed before Jesus and told Him he was ready to do anything necessary to find eternal life. Jesus told him to sell his possessions, give the money to the poor, and to follow Him. The young man found this to be too great a sacrifice. He turned his back on Jesus and walked away.

Following Jesus, serving Him, fulfilling whatever

missions He directs us to is not always going to be easy. We can sing hymns such as "There Is Joy in Serving Jesus," but while there is joy, there also is sacrifice. They go together.

Our overall mission—to emulate Jesus as we serve Him—is not impossible, merely difficult. But its rewards greatly outweigh its costs.

# Where death is often preferred to life.

Humberto Noble Alexander stood naked and freezing before his captors in the stark, slab-gray interrogation room. Fairness and justice meant nothing here.

It was 1962 . . . in Castro's Cuba.

Falsely accused of conspiracy to assassinate the Communist dictator, this young preacher would spend the next twenty-two years as a political prisoner in one of the most inhumane and brutal prison systems on earth.

*I Will Die Free* is a stunning testimony of persecution and perseverance that will awe and inspire all who read it.

Tortured in a Cuban prison for preaching the gospel, Noble Alexander refused to recant and found strength in his cry . . .

**I WILL DIE FREE**

**NOBLE ALEXANDER** with **KAY D. RIZZO**

**US$9.95/Cdn$12.45. Paper. ISBN 0-8163-1044-0**

Order from your local Christian bookstore.

# IF IT WERE A NIGHTMARE, YOU COULD WAKE UP!

**B**ut for Chanla and his family, the nightmare was real.

On April 17, 1975, a savage killing machine known as the Khmer Rouge drove this well-respected family, along with thousands of others, from their home in Phnom Penh to the rice fields, where they were forced to endure backbreaking labor amid unspeakable horrors.

*Salvation in the Killing Fields*, by Aileen Ludington, is the gut-wrenching story of one family's desperate and deadly flight to freedom, and their life-changing encounter with Jesus Christ.

You will search long and hard for a story that can shock, move, and inspire you the way this one will. Don't miss out on the experience! Get *Salvation in the Killing Fields* today!

**US$9.95/Cdn$12.45. Paper, 192 pages.**
*Please photocopy and complete form below.*

---

❑ *Salvation in the Killing Fields:* US$9.95/Cdn$12.45.
Please add applicable sales tax and 15% (US$2.50 minimum) to cover postage and handling.

Name _____
Address _____
City _____
State _____ Zip _____

Price      $ _____
Postage    $ _____
Sales Tax  $ _____
TOTAL      $ _____

Order from your local Christian bookstore or ABC Mailing Service, P.O. Box 7000, Boise, Idaho 83707. Prices subject to change without notice. Make check payable to Pacific Press.

© 1990 Pacific Press Publishing Association 2227

In the midst of unthinkable atrocities, one family found...

**SALVATION IN THE KILLING FIELDS**

AILEEN LUDINGTON AND DARRYL LUDINGTON